GOD'S HEART – YOUR HANDS

This One's for You, Caregiver

by

Laurie Zurinsky

PRESS

Dedication

This book is dedicated to the memory of my dad,
Bob Mickelson, a lover of people.

Contents

A Personal Note..ix

1. January – Decisions Decisions....................11
2. February – Pressing On..............................33
3. March – Boomers.....................................51
4. April – The Buck $ Stops Here...................73
5. May – Gimme a Break..............................93
6. June – Dust Bunnies................................111
7. July – The Fam.......................................127
8. August – Day by Day...............................143
9. September – History Lessons....................163
10. October – My Way or Yahweh?................181
11. November – Focus 199
12. December – Pause 217

Notes 235

Acknowledgements....................................239

A Personal Note...

Beloved Caregiver,

You have made a choice. You have conquered the temptation to live life in the fast lane and have opted instead for a life of service. Good for you!

Consider yourself blessed. For this journey will make you grow in depth and status.

"Status?" you ask. "What status can be gained by spoonfeeding and changing diapers?" Well, I can tell you right now – you are big in *my* eyes!

Together we are going to walk through 1 Corinthians, Chapter 13 – The LOVE CHAPTER. God has a special message for you there. He knows and cares about what you are going through. You are not alone.

We will look at real-life issues: discouragement, money, the family and isolation. Some of the situations may remind you of somebody. It might even be you!

Hopefully these anecdotes, prayers and verses will help you get through the days ahead.

You are needed, respected and appreciated.

Love,

Laurie

ONE

DECISIONS DECISIONS

*If I speak with human eloquence and angelic ecstasy
but don't love, I'm nothing but the creaking of a rusty gate.
If I speak God's Word with power, revealing all his myster-
ies and making everything plain as day, and if I have faith
that says to a mountain, "Jump," and it jumps,
but I don't love, I'm nothing.
If I give everything I own to the poor and I even go to the
stake to be burned as a martyr, but I don't love, I've gotten
nowhere. So, no matter what I say, what I believe, and
what I do, I'm bankrupt without love.*

January 1

We've got it all under control, don't we? After all, we live in the Computer Age. At the touch of a button we connect with Bankers and Stock Brokers who do our bidding. We contact others through Cyber Space via the Internet, Cell Phones and Walkie-Talkies. We send flowers and candies 'online' to cover the appropriate holiday gifts. In fact, we hardly ever have to look people in the eye.

We take pills to enhance our moods, our appetites, and our sex lives.

Yet, we are impotent when it comes to the 'biggie': the fact that people get sick and die. And there is no computer or pill that can help us to avoid that unavoidable truth.

What then do we do when faced with people who are suffering? When the rubber meets the road – when we fight the huge inner battles – we discover that our character is on the line.

Oh, Caregiver, you have fought the temptation to look the other way. You have made the wise choice to minister to others. Painstakingly. Selflessly.

In the days and weeks, even years ahead, you will grow and grow in love for your God and for humanity in ways that cannot be explained.

Godspeed as you travail this rocky path.

January 2

Let's Get Moving...

Ummm, Dad, let's put the clothes INTO the suitcase, ok?

Yes, we'll take both of your cars with us.

Wow! You know you have about 6 months worth of newspapers here?

Yes, we'll bring the cat.

We'll keep your money in the same bank it's in now. Don't worry about your money anymore, Dad. You don't need to sit with your calculator every day. I will take over paying your bills. I'll make sure that your accounts stay in order.

That's an interesting way to hang your shirts – with the hangar poked right through the back like that.

Oh, Lord! The more we dig in – Ahhhhg!

Yes, Dad, you and Mom will still be together. We'll *all* be together.

All the time. From now on. All for one and one for all. Day in. Day out.

Yikes!

January 3

Some days I just don't want to get out of bed. My mind is stressed. My body is tired. How can I properly care for the aged when I can barely move myself?

Then, I remember my friend, Erma. Eighty-seven years young, this vital lady encourages me to keep going. Watching her is like taking a multiple vitamin for both heart and soul.

When Erma is feeling weak, and she's got to get going, she'll joke, "I told my legs, 'It's time to go now', and they answered back, 'We'll go when we get good and ready to go!'"

She'll then ask assistance from whoever is nearby to help get her out of the chair. And off she goes: To the lunchroom. To church. To the neighbors. Such enthusiasm! Ministering to others!

When I'm the one who is asked to help Erma out of the chair, I fully realize that Erma is really helping me!

"So let's not allow ourselves to get fatigued doing good." Galatians 6:9

January 4

A scoffing world is looking on,
The furnace glows with furious heat.
The test is real, the foe is near,
Waiting to witness my retreat.

Hosts of evil gather round me,
The Son of God seems lost to view.
Oh, for faith to meet the crisis;
Oh, for the courage to go through!

What, this sudden sweet empow'ring?
Whence, this strange, exultant cry?
If my God comes not, I'll trust Him,
Though to trust Him means to die!
Margaret Denison Armstrong [1]

January 5

Little Ruthie sat in her wheelchair, excited about being at the symphony. She had never been away from home much. It was difficult to take her places, as she was unable to cooperate in her own care and transportation. She had Rett's Syndrome and her future was unsure. So her dad was determined to make this evening work. He had purchased two tickets and could think of no one he would love to spend the time with more than his seven-year-old daughter.

A wonderful piano soloist would be here tonight. The evening promised to be a grand one. As the orchestra warmed up Ruthie happily sat and watched the people file in. What an event this would be!

At a pause in the music, Ruthie squealed with joy! Her father hugged her. The couple sitting in front of them turned, scowled and asked them to leave.

Well, it was understandable. After all, it was a public event, and the world just doesn't get it and doesn't care. They did not understand God's heart. Ruthie's daddy decided to forgive them right then and there.

At church the following morning, Ruthie did it again. She squealed with joy over something or someone she had seen. Ruthie's dad smiled and patted her hand. But the lady in the row in front of them turned to scowl.

Not here, too, Lord! Not here, too! The father's broken heart cried.

> *Oh, Father God. I remember the sadness I felt when I learned that Jesus' own people killed Him. And now we are His people and we kill Him, too. Change us, Lord. Remind us Who we belong to.*

January 6

Don't make important decisions in a **FOG**!
Fear
Obligation
Guilt

The only worthwhile motivator is LOVE.

This is my concern...

_____

_____

_____

_____

_____

_____

January 7

The hallmark of our retirement is – we can't make a decision anymore! *Tim Jacobson*

It's fun to joke about old age, but it is true – retirement is not always what it's pegged up to be. You only retire from your job. You don't get to retire from your infirmities. In fact, the illnesses seem to be on a roll!

It is possible that this one you are caring for is suffering from extreme disappointment. The 'golden years' have not been golden at all.

Aim for the heart, dear Caregiver. Aim for the heart.

"Your very lives are a letter that anyone can read by just looking at you. Christ himself wrote it – not with ink, but with God's living Spirit; not chiseled into stone, but carved into human lives... It's written with Spirit on spirit, his life on our lives!"
2 Corinthians 3:2-3, 6b

January 8

He was there when she was born. He placed her in a wonderful family. He watched carefully as she played with her little friends.

He guided her into her marriage to a godly young man. He was there as each of her children was born.

He put joy in her heart as she ministered to her family, her church, and her community in His name.

When she was widowed, He stayed by her side. Through the sorrow, the loneliness, He was there. He provided comfort to her soul when she wept.

He encouraged her as she put together a new life. He loved to watch her as she volunteered at the local hospital;

as she babysat her grandchildren; as she helped her elderly neighbor.

The hairs on her head are numbered by Him. He knows all the days of her life. He loves her so. She belongs to Him.

And now *she* is the elderly one. *She* needs help. God looked far and wide for the perfect caregiver for her.

And He chose you.

"Do your best. Work from the heart for your real Master, for God..." Colossians 3:23

January 9

Are you tired, friend? Feeling isolated?

Focus on this: You are doing God's work when you care for this one in need.

Pay attention to your relationship with Him. The rest will follow.

Remember! You can't spill out what you are not carrying!

"... keep your eyes on Jesus, who both began and finished this race we're in. Study how he did it. Because he never lost sight of where he was headed – that exhilarating finish in and with God – he could put up with anything along the way: cross, shame, whatever. And now he's there, in the place of honor, right alongside God. When you find yourselves flagging in your faith, go over that story again, item by item, that long litany of hostility he plowed through. That will shoot adrenaline into your souls!" Hebrews 12:2-3

January 10

Decide to be Sober – But Not Somber!

It was a 30' cabin cruiser, two stories high with plenty of room for everyone. We were cruising on a beautiful day. The weather was balmy; warm breeze across the hull.

I sat with my legs over the side – getting some sun. Steve sat beside me in his wheelchair, enjoying the ride.

A friend asked Steve (in a baby voice), "Are you cold?" Steve, unable to talk, shook his head "no."

It seemed that everyone loved Steve, but many babied him. He was in a terrible predicament for sure, a neuro-degenerative disease ravaging his body. But his mind was there. All there.

In an attempt to validate his adulthood, I took a chance: Like I would rib anyone else, I said in a smart-alecky way, "Well, it's a good thing you're not cold, 'cause I'm not giv-ing up my spot in the sun!" I slowly turned toward Steve for his response.

He turned, smiled, and burst out laughing – Steve style – mouth wide open! He liked being treated normally!

Then he took it even farther. He turned his wheelchair, bent down, grabbed his pants legs, gave them a yank, and swung his legs over the edge of the boat alongside mine.

I teased, "Well, that's great – but you've got long pants on! You can't get a tan with long pants on!"

Again, he responded with humor. He reached down and pulled up the legs of his sweats above his knees. This guy is a good sport! Everyone needs a laugh once in awhile!

Wouldn't you know it? We didn't get a tan that day. As soon as we were both situated, the boat turned, and our sun-source went away.

But – the *Son*-source was there in full power! Jesus was cruising right along with us – and I think I heard Him chuckle, too!

January 11

Are we crazy?

There are those out there in the big wide world who think it's nuts for us to spend our time spoon-feeding someone who forgets our names more often than not. "It's not good for you," they say. "You shouldn't tie yourself down like this. Life is too short."
One point of view.
But in God's Word, the message is so very different:

"This is how we've come to understand and experience love: Christ sacrificed his life for us. This is why we ought to live sacrificially for our fellow believers, and not just be out for ourselves. If you see some brother or sister in need and have the means to do something about it but turn a cold shoulder and do nothing, what happens to God's love? It disappears. And you made it disappear.

"My dear children, let's not just talk about love; let's practice real love. This is the only way we'll know we're living truly, living in God's reality."
1 John 3:17, 18

So, let's go for it, Caregivers! Let's take a walk on the wild side! Self-abandonment isn't crazy at all!

January 12

Where There's Room in the Heart, There's Room in the Home.

Maybe I should invite this suffering one to stay with me...

_____

_____

_____

_____

_____

_____

January 13

Talk talk talk talk talk.

Remember when he was a DJ on the radio?

Remember when he used to relate his entire life history to anybody who would listen? The gas station attendant – the guy in the elevator?

Remember all his jokes?

And now, he can no longer put together a complete sentence. Oh, he harkens back to his old 'standbys,' the witty sayings from his past: "Looks good to me!" or "Let's go for it!" "You got it, Babe."

But it's gone.

He has this look in his eye. A sweet longing. An 'I want to know you and to be known by you' look. And I am gripped with fear when I realize that my Dad can no longer be known.

What horror! To not be able to get across a simple thought like, "Pass the butter, please."

Oh, Lord, what shall I do? Is it possible for me to take care of him with his dementia?

He tried to explain something to me the other day. It went something like, "So, when we use the whichamagidget for the thingy – then what'd ya get?" At first I didn't know how to respond. Then he looked at me with a wry grin and said with humor, "You don't get it, do you?" I laughed lightly, "Dad, I don't have a clue!" He shared in my laughter.

Someone needs to be there to laugh with him – or cry with him – for the rest of his life!

God, please guide this caregiver as she makes the big decisions. Let her feel Your hand upon her life and the life of this infirmed one. Amen.

January 14

Helping the doctor make decisions. It's an important part of the job.

FAX: Dear Dr. Hanson. Mom hasn't been eating well lately. She's losing weight. I think her teeth hurt, but she won't admit it.

Dr. Hanson: So, Mrs. Hardy, let me look in your mouth.

Mom: In my mouth? There's nothing wrong with my mouth!

Dr. Hanson: Uh huh... Now open wide! You need to see a dentist, Ma'am, that tooth has got to come out!

FAX: Mom's been real depressed lately. Maybe she needs some meds.

Dr. Hanson: So, Mrs. Hardy, how have you been feeling lately?

Mom: Everything is just fine, Doctor.

Dr. Hanson: OK then, I have a prescription I'd like for

you to try.

FAX: Mom isn't getting any exercise. She's got no energy.
Dr. Hanson: So, are you getting any exercise?
Mom: Sure! Every day!
Dr. Hanson: Good! I'd like for you to walk with your son every other day around the mall, ok?

~~~

FAX: Thank you, Doctor. Things are going better now.
Mom: That doctor sure knows what he's doing, doesn't he?

January 15

Anxiety washed over me. What are You thinking, God? I can't take care of someone with Alzheimer's!

My insides were screaming! NO! I just can't do it!

But then, Lord, you gently nudged me. You asked me if we could spend some quality time together. And I discovered on my knees what I could not see when I was on the run.

I saw my mom, someone I love a lot. Someone YOU love a lot! She's helpless now. And the answer was obvious: Of course. We will minister to Mom for the rest of her life. And somehow, the love will overcome the trouble.

"Get down on your knees before the Master; it's the only way you'll get on your feet." James 4:10

January 16

He calls me by the wrong name all the time. And I am his only child!

HE DOESN'T CALL MY NAME AT ALL. AND I AM THE AUTHOR OF HIS LIFE! PERSPECTIVE.

But....but You are God! You are all-powerful! All-knowing. I'm a wimp! I look at the big picture and faint!

PICK UP THE BIBLE.

What could the Bible possibly have to say about my situation?

"My grace is enough; it's all you need.
My strength comes into its own in your weakness.

Once I heard that, I was glad to let it happen. I quit focusing on the handicap and began appreciating the gift. It was a case of Christ's strength moving in on my weakness. Now I take limitations in stride, and with good cheer, these limitations that cut me down to size – abuse, accidents, opposition, bad breaks. I just let Christ take over! And so the weaker I get, the stronger I become." 2 Corinthians 12:9-10

(I should have come to You a long time ago, Lord.)

January 17

Are those snapshots of Dad?

Yes they are.

See? That's the two of you. He's bouncing you on his knee.

Remember this one? He's chaperoning your first dance.

Remember the tears? He's walking you down the aisle.

He's always been there for you, hasn't he?

Turn the page, Ahhh! He's planning his retirement. The grandchildren. The travel. He deserves it.

Turn again. It's Dad and you and the doctor. Looks like Alzheimer's.

Unfair, you say? Oh yeah. It's unfair.

How long has this been going on, you ask?

Child, it's been happening right under your nose. But you couldn't have known.

What do the next pages look like?

Well, let's look in on those...

Here are you and your dad, continuing your relationship. The colors are not so rosy, but see how the tints and hues are deeper.

See here – he's laughing. You may not know why, but somehow you still make him laugh.

Look how he's watching you – studying you – almost looking right though you – as you cut his meat into bite-size pieces.

Here – He's still walking with you – with a little help.

Don't worry. You're still connected.

New pictures. New seasons. Beautiful. Loving.

January 18

Even if you're on the right track – you get run over if you just sit there. *Will Rogers*

Lord, will You light a fire under me? I have this decision to make...

_____

_____

_____

_____

_____

January 19

"Be kind to me, God –
I'm in deep, deep trouble again.
I've cried my eyes out;
I feel hollow inside.
My life leaks away, groan by groan;
my years fade out in sighs.
My troubles have worn me out,
turned my bones to powder." Psalms 31:9-12

Oh Lord! Is this how this suffering one feels?

January 20

Good morning, child. I've been thinking about you a lot lately; in fact you are always on My mind.

I've decided that you should do something new today. I want you to take off the mask.

Oh, I know. It is difficult to let others see you. But don't worry. After all, they won't be looking at a serial killer! – Just you in your weakness.

You see, there is another who is deciding whether or not to become a caregiver. She is coming into this kicking and screaming – just like you did! – and I want her to know that she is not alone.

It is no accident that you will run into her today.

Be honest. Show her the love. Help her to decide.

January 21

*Lord, I'm trying to decide whether **I** need a care-*
giver!

I'm forgetful. I tell the same story over and over again until my kids roll their eyes. "You're just like Grandma," they say. I'm even spelling words wrong now. I do weird things.

Take yesterday...

I was driving down the freeway. As usual, I was late for an appointment, so I 'primped' a little in the car. I checked my lipstick and eye makeup.

I pulled my sunglasses down to get a good look in the rearview mirror – just to be sure my face was in order. (Everybody does that, don't they?) When I went to pull my glasses back on – I got the little nose thingies stuck in my nostrils! The driver in the car next to me tried to pretend he didn't see the whole thing. And I just burst out laughing! I laughed all the way to my exit!

So, God, what'd ya think? Is this caregiver losing it?

January 22

Denial is not a river in Egypt. *Steve Brown*

Denial is not some far away thing that we don't have to deal with. It's close up and personal and we are surrounded by it.

Denial is a gut-deep 'not wanting' of something so personal, so hurtful, that it gets pushed to the back of the mind, into the darkest recesses. People deny suffering and death – their own and their loved ones'.

Some people, when in denial, act angry and haughty and

proud. Others just avoid the pain through drugs or alcohol. Others yet just don't show up.

They are driven by fear, Beloved Caregiver; fear of that which *you* have decided to meet head-on.

Love is the key. Love in response to a loving God.

> *"There is no room in love for fear. Well-formed love banishes fear. Since fear is crippling, a fearful life – fear of death, fear of judgment – is one not yet fully formed in love. We though, are going to love – love and be loved. First we were loved, now we love. He loved us first." 1 John 4:18-19*

January 23

I'm trading my sorrows.
I'm trading my shame.
I'm laying them down
For the joy of the Lord.

I'm trading my sickness.
I'm trading my pain.
I'm laying them down
For the joy of the Lord... *Darrell Evans* [2]

Lord, that this one I care for would decide for You today – and feel the relief that only You can give. That suffering would be traded for joy as Your healing hand covers the brokenness. I pray for redemption, O God.

January 24

"If any of you want to serve me, then follow me. Then you'll be where I am, ready to serve at a moment's notice. The Father will honor and reward anyone who serves me." John 12:26

God, as I serve You today I offer up this prayer...

_____

_____

_____

_____

_____

_____

January 25

This is just great, Lord. So, now what am I supposed to do? I mentioned to her that we could get her an apartment in one of those nice retirement villages, and it went over like a lead balloon.

She is insisting that she lives right next door! I am getting panicky!

BUT SHE HAS AGREED TO MOVE?

Well, yes. But on her terms!

MAYBE THEY ARE MY TERMS, TOO.

~~~

There is no reason to believe that parents would want to be uprooted from their comfort zone unless they can be placed in close proximity to you.

January 26

For years they had been on stage. A family of talented singers, dancers and actors, they used their talents for God.

Then Vorece had a stroke. As she drove the family car down a busy street, the stroke hit her, and she crashed into a telephone pole.

"She doesn't know who she is," warned the doctor. "I cannot guarantee that she will come back fully."

The family, church and community prayed for Vorece. In His infinite mercy, God answered, and she was soon back on her feet. Completely, they thought.

Several months later, Vorece, her daughter and grand-daughter were asked to perform at a fund-raiser for the local Christian school. They chose a beautifully choreographed piece from a Broadway show.

Vorece came in right on cue. Down the center aisle, dressed to the nines, parasol over her shoulder. She swept through the crowd, nodding "hello," getting to the front just in time. As she joined her daughter and granddaughter, the three were to twirl their parasols, turn to the audience and begin their routine together.

Thing is, Vorece forgot to turn to the audience. She twirled in a complete circle! She did her dance with her back to the crowd!

The performance was a smashing success! Not because it was done well, but because it was done in love. She loved the community – and they loved her back.

That's what it's all about, right?

January 27

Susan got Mom ready to go that morning. She counted out her meds, fixed her breakfast, helped her bathe, curled her hair and dressed her in a pretty outfit.

She checked Mom's mail, pulling out the bills that had to be paid. Then off they went to church, Susan pushing Mom's wheelchair.

It was Service Day that Sunday – a celebration of the congregants who spent their time in service for others.

Pastor asked those who were in the nursing profession to stand. Everyone applauded. He asked the nursery workers to stand. Again, applause. Then he asked the caregivers to stand – the ones who worked in nursing homes, assisted living homes, or cared for someone at home.

As he spoke, Mom elbowed Susan in the side and whispered, "Let's stand up, Susan. We're both caregivers!"

January 28

To punish me for my contempt for authority, Fate has made me an authority myself. *Albert Einstein*

> *Lord, yesterday I was her child. Today I am her caregiver. What irony! I'm not sure I am comfortable with this shift in responsibility, but I choose to give it a try. Not because of 'fate,' God, but because I trust Your love will carry the day.*

January 29

Does it really matter why he is in this condition? Did his drinking/drug-taking/over-eating/fast-driving/dare-devil-ing/suicide-attempting lifestyle put him here?

When the infirmity is the result of self-destructive behavior it would be easy for us to become self-righteous and let him know that he was wrong. We would be technically right, but is it worth bruising his soul over?

With everything that is in us, let's determine that it's OK to care for him – sans the angry bitterness that often comes in this package of care-giving.

Let's concentrate on the positive – we have an opportunity to introduce another soul to Jesus Christ. It just might be time for this suffering one to make a *good* decision.

January 30

> *"Listen carefully. Unless a grain of wheat is buried in the ground, dead to the world, it is never any more than a grain of wheat. But if it is buried, it sprouts and reproduces itself many times over. In the same way, anyone who holds on to life just as it is destroys that life. But if you let it go, reckless in your love, you'll have it forever, real and external."*
> *John 12:24-25*

Lord, I have to set myself aside in this way...

_____

_____

_____

_____

_____

_____

January 31

He probably didn't want to live here. He would like to be on his own. But he has accepted it.

If he could, he would go back in time - recapture his past.

"Back in the days," he says all day long.

He tells you stories about his hometown. How he would walk down the street and it would be "Hey, Bob!" "How's it goin', Bob?" It was sort of like in the 'Cheers' song – "Where everybody knows your name." The problem is – that nobody knows his name anymore – except you.

And he is grateful for you.

What a privilege to serve him now, with his aging mind and body. Because of you, he is not alone. He has a friend.

God has inserted you into his troubled life to nurture and protect him. Amazing!

TWO

PRESSING ON

Love never gives up.

February 1

Discouragement creeps in. It's inevitable. You get deflated.

It's all about perspective. From your end, you cannot see any progress. The sick get sicker. The suffering continues.

Please take heart, Caregiver! Recognize that your view is limited. You see one side of the tapestry – the tangled up one.

But eternity will expose the topside. And it will be beautiful! The bright yellows of the happy days, the purple passions, and even your 'blues' will unfold into a portrait of love.

So, look ahead! This hard time – with respect to eternity – will only make the weaving a bit richer, deeper, more complete.

God is doing a work here!

February 2

Hey, Dad, you're walking kind of funny. Do your feet hurt? How about we take a look?

Oh, Lord! I've never seen anything like this! His nails are completely curled over the top and digging in under his toes!

~~~

Know what, Dad? I bought this special shampoo. It will take care of that dry patch on your head. That's right. Why don't you come on over to the sink, and I'll just wash your hair for you? Sure! I've got time.

If you hold the towel over your eyes, Dad, then I can rinse the soap off your head. No, hold it against your eyes.

Oh, Lord, he doesn't understand.

Here, let me put it in just the right position, ok?

~~~

Three years, huh? Wow! That's a long time to go without a shower!

~~~

Guess what, Dad? I know you don't like the shower, so Rich is gonna help you get into the bathtub! It'll be ok, Dad. No, I won't come in there. Just you guys.

~~~

Hey, there, Handsome! Now that's more like it! You look like a million bucks.

February 3

There is no wilderness so terrible, so beautiful, so arid and fruitful as the wilderness of compassion. It is the only desert that shall truly flourish like the lily... *Thomas Merton* [3]

She had Parkinson's. She could no longer walk, and her hallucinations were severe. It was hard to tell whether her hands were trembling from the disease or from the fear.

Her loving husband, her caregiver, held her hand and spoke in soothing tones. They'd been here before. He'd seen the panic. He'd heard the violent conversations with the 'other' people in the room. He just sat with her. And held her.

She had been in someone else's care for the past few weeks: First at the hospital, then at the nursing home. They just couldn't get her medications nailed down. Nothing seemed to be helping.

So he brought her home.

And he would begin each day with gratitude in his heart.

Thankful for the 'good' years they'd had together. Determined to make the best of an uncertain future.

February 4

Fear turns spiritual muscle into mental mush. *David Erickson*

> *"So be content with who you are, and don't put on airs. God's strong hand is on you; he'll promote you at the right time. Live carefree before God; he is most careful with you.*
>
> *Keep a cool head. Stay alert. The Devil is poised to pounce, and would like nothing better than to catch you napping. Keep your guard up. You're not the only ones plunged into these hard times. It's the same with Christians all over the world. So keep a firm grip on the faith. The suffering won't last forever. It won't be long before this generous God who has great plans for us in Christ – eternal and glorious plans they are! – will have you put together and on your feet for good. He gets the last word; yes, he does." 1 Peter 5:6-12*

February 5

"Ed! You are putting your sweater on upside down!"
"No! Not that way! Do it right!"
Jesse intervened. "He doesn't know how."
"Well, he knew how yesterday!"
"Look, it really doesn't matter because he doesn't know how today. Ed, it's ok. Don't give up. Here, let me help you."

Was that a glimmer of hope in the old man's eyes?

"There you go, Ed. Yep, it's on right now. Lookin' good, man."

(All the time trying to keep a straight face. Ed had on two pairs of pants.)

February 6

Wisdom rejects mediocrity. Do your Best!

Oh, God, I have a confession. I feel like giving up sometimes when...

_____

_____

_____

_____

_____

_____

February 7

It was Easter Sunday. The choir, standing along the risers, waited for their esteemed director, Clint. They had been rehearsing for several weeks and felt confident that this cantata would be the best one they had ever done together. The lyrics and music were beautifully written, and under Clint's passionate direction, the whole performance would be moving. They were sure of that.

What they hadn't anticipated, however, was the strong emotional reaction they would have when Clint took his baton in hand.

They had heard he'd been to the doctor. It was rumored that it might be Parkinson's. He'd even had to miss several rehearsals, asking others to sit in for him during his absence.

When Clint came to stand before them, there was no room left for speculation. His hands were trembling, his gait unsteady, and worse, there were tears streaming down his cheeks. He had been given very bad news, indeed. This would be the last concert he would direct.

This vital musician, director, concert pianist, would soon be losing control of parts of his body, and possibly his mind.

Director and choir alike cried through the music, along with several congregation members as they 'caught on.'

It was a beautiful ceremony: A celebration of his accomplishments in life, and a compassion for what was to come, all lifted up to God – an offering of thanksgiving for the assurance and the truth of the Resurrection.

Lord, help me to understand, as caregiver to this elderly one, that what is left of his hopes and aspirations lie in You. You are his future.

February 8

Whoops! Dad, you have to knock before you come into my bathroom!

Oh God, help me to laugh at the small stuff.

February 9

Remember not only to say the right thing in the right place, but far more difficult still, to leave unsaid the wrong thing at the tempting moment. *Benjamin Franklin*

Easier said than done. Short of all that self-control, remember that if you blow it, and get this suffering one angry at you (easy to do, huh?), ask for forgiveness. If you get mad at her, forgive! That way, your relationship will heal up quickly.

> *"Go ahead and be angry. You do well to be angry – but don't use your anger as fuel for revenge. And don't stay angry. Don't go to bed angry. Don't give the devil that kind of foothold in your life."*
> *Ephesians 4:26-27*

February 10

There is nothing in the universe that I fear, except that I shall not know all my duty, or shall fail to do it. *Mary Lyon*

Any extra little thing that I'm asked to do seems overwhelming when I'm this spent. I get weepy, irritable. But this is my job – and with God's help, I won't give up. Because Love never gives up!

February 11

She is suffering from depression.

She won't leave her room. Worse yet – except to use the bathroom, she won't even leave her easy chair! The TV blares at her all day long. That's her input.

She's not fond of other people. Or activities. Or reading. Or exercise. Or her medication. So she just doesn't do those things.

She has many illnesses – her body is aging rapidly.

She feels like she has nothing to live for. She has hit a brick wall. A dead end.

It seems pretty hopeless.

As her caregiver, what can you do? You cannot force her

to live her remaining years to the fullest. But maybe, just maybe you can lead her to the way of Life Abundant.

Introducing her to Jesus Christ is the answer. You know that for certain. He can comfort her in ways that are impossible for you! He can give her a peace that passes understanding. He can give her a future.

This job of caregiver has many faces, doesn't it?

February 12

One more day –
One more clean shirt.
Grandma Garrity

Today, I am going to count my blessings...

_____

_____

_____

_____

_____

_____

February 13

Picture with me if you can,
A little girl in a younger land,
Running, playing, laughing, growing stronger.

Now the aging limbs have failed,
And the rosy cheeks have paled.
Look behind the lines 'til you remember.

She's still the same girl, flying down the hill.
She's still the same girl, memories vivid still.
Listen to her story and her eyes will glow.
She's still the same girl, and she needs you so.

Picture with me if you will,
A long white dress and a wedding veil,
Two young dreamers pledge their love together.

Now her lifelong friend is gone,
And she spends her days alone.
Look behind the lines 'til you remember.

She's still the same girl, walking down the aisle.
She's still the same girl, with the shining smile.
Listen to her story and her eyes will glow.
She's still the same girl, and she needs you so.

She's still the same girl, wiser for the years.
She's still the same girl, stronger for the tears.
Listen to her story and your heart will grow.
She's still the same girl, and you need her so. *Twila Paris* [4]

Lord, let me never forget that this little lady was once just like me. Help me to pay attention to her stories as I tend to her daily needs. Remind me to listen – really listen to her. She has something to teach me.

O God, help me to treat her the way I want to be treated in my 'Twilight' years.

February 14
Valentine's Day

Oh, Caregiver, no matter what is happening today, keep in mind: This really is a love fest!

> *"My beloved friends, let us continue to love each other since love comes from God. Everyone who loves is born of God and experiences a relationship with God. The person who refuses to love doesn't know the first thing about God, because God is love – so you can't know him if you don't love." 1 John 4:7-8*

February 15

In For a Penny, In For a Pound...

Oh, Dad. Look at you. So frightened. So lost.

The fear in you is contagious, you know. I tremble when you tremble.

You are so confused. You bump around the house as though you don't know what to do next. I am so sorry this move has bewildered you so.

Did we make a mistake? Should we have left you where you were? You are so depressed. And you can barely get your words out now. What have I done?

> *Lord, I fear for my dad. He has lost his independence and he is taking it so badly! He trusted me, God – that I would do the right thing for him. I am honored by his trust. I am determined to give him a life of quality. I just can't let him down!*

Will You help him? Will You give me words of comfort for him? Will You teach me how to honor him back?

February 16

Dear friends, do you think you'll get anywhere in this if you learn all the right words but never do anything? Does merely talking about faith indicate that a person really has it? For instance, you come upon an old friend dressed in rags and half-starved and say, "Good morning, friend! Be clothed in Christ! Be filled with the Holy Spirit!" and walk off without providing so much as a coat or a cup of soup – where does that get you? Isn't it obvious that God-talk without God-acts is outrageous nonsense?

I can already hear one of you agreeing by saying, "Sounds good. You take care of the faith department, I'll handle the works department."

Not so fast. You can no more show me your works apart from your faith than I can show you my faith apart from my works. Faith and works, works and faith, fit together hand in glove. James 2:14-18

February 17

We had another big argument today, Lord. She keeps insisting that she can drive the car, and it's so obvious that she can't. I told her that I would drive her where she needs to go. But she won't listen to me. She wants to hang on to this little bit of independence at other people's risk. I am so angry with her!

YOU ARE RIGHT ABOUT EVERYTHING YOU SAID. BUT, DON'T YOU SEE? YOU ARE *BOTH* SUFFERING FROM A HEART PROBLEM.
HER PAIN? THAT HER LIFE IS SLIPPING AWAY.
YOUR PAIN? THAT HER LIFE IS SLIPPING AWAY.
YOU REALLY SHOULD BE HOLDING HANDS.

February 18

"It is absolutely clear that God has called you to a free life. Just make sure that you don't use this freedom as an excuse to do whatever you want to do and destroy your freedom. Rather, use your freedom to serve one another in love; that's how freedom grows. For everything we know about God's Word is summed up in a single sentence: Love others as you love yourself." Galatians 5:13-14

Lord, I need Your love for others. Especially...

_____

_____

_____

_____

_____

_____

February 19

Fear Stops Life – Not Death

"Grandpa! Grandpa! Calm down! We just went to the grocery store. We were only gone for an hour."

"Well, Grandma isn't going to fall down! She's sitting in the chair watching TV."

"Yes, I know, you've been guarding her the whole time."

~~~

"Yes, the power went out this morning. But we're all set. We hooked up the generator, and the heat is turned back on."

"What? No, it's not cold in here. Actually, it's 75 degrees."

"No, you're not going to get hypothermia."

~~~

"No, Grandpa. Jack won't bite you. He's known you since he was a puppy. He's a good, gentle dog."

~~~

"Don't worry. You can sit back in the seat. Just relax. We won't let the trucks hit us. They do whiz on by though, don't they?"

~~~

"Don't you think it's fun to be out on the boat? Grandpa, why are you making Grandma untie her shoelaces? Oh, I see. Just in case the boat sinks and she has to swim." (Of course, if she swam it would *really* be a miracle. She's never known how to swim.)

Oh Lord, what can we do to quell his fears?

February 20

It was one of those days. Taking care of Mom was overwhelming sometimes, and Kathy didn't know if she had the patience to carry on.

When she asked her mom to open her mouth for a bite of food, she was ignored. She chewed up her meds and spit them out. She forgot to mention that she had to go to the bathroom. It was just one of those days.

Kathy decided to get them out of the house for a while.

"Hurry up, Mom! The car is running."

Then she appeared. Mom. All decked out. Nice little dress. White gloves. Handbag over her arm. And both eyebrows done up nicely in bright pink lipstick!

(Is there such a word as bitter-funny?)

February 21

"You work with the elderly? Whoa! That's tough, huh? I mean, like, what kind of future is there in that line of work?"

(Some people just don't get it.)

Doing really hard work with people in need? There's a **great** future in that! My future **and** their futures. **Mega** futures!

I can touch every one of them with the Gospel of Jesus Christ.

February 22

A handle from the Bible:

"Dignify those who are down on their luck; you'll feel good – that's what God does." Psalms 41:1

February 23

Real knowledge:
Blushes before pride
Bows before love

Help me, God, to be a 'Smarty.' (in a good way)

Don't let me get prideful when...

_____

_____

_____

_____

_____

_____

February 24

"OK Mom. Here we are back home. It's been a big day, hasn't it?"

"Big day?"

"Well sure! We've been to the bank, the grocery store, your little granddaughter's birthday party! We've been real gadabouts today!"

"We sure have. Say, who are you?"

"I'm Connie, Mom! Connie."

"You are one of my kids, aren't you?"

"Yeah, Mom. I am."

*Lord, bless the caregiver who gets no recognition. Lift her up as she does her work 'anonymously.' Remind her that even though she has accepted her no-name role, **You know who she is and what she is doing**! Keep her going, God. Amen.*

February 25

Every year Glenn threw himself a birthday party. I mean, a BIG birthday party. The whole church was invited! There would be refreshments and music! His nephew, a concert pianist, would give a concert.

Glenn would wear his tennis shoes and a baseball cap. He would get up in front of everybody and do a little shuffle. At ninety years old – he was dancing!

His legs and hands shook from Parkinson's disease, but it didn't get him down. Glenn was a confident man.

He knew that he belonged to Jesus. And even though he loved his life, he was excited to meet the Lord face to face. He had no fear of death.

He always was a generous man. He sought out those in need. He gave the last of his fortunes to the church, holding out just enough to get by in the assisted living place he now called his home.

By anyone's accounting, Glenn had it all under control – he and his God.

Glenn held on to just one earthly desire: companionship. He still needed people.

Who could deny him that?

The two most important words in ministry: Be There.

February 26

Oh, Lord! Look at Dad! He's taking a walk outside! He's talking to his cat. Oh, how he loves her!

Remember the day we gave her to him? How she fell asleep on his chest? He was needed again.

Thank you, Lord, that you gave us these two little acres – just so my Dad could wander a bit.

Being grateful for the small stuff. It's a good way to keep from giving up!

February 27

"If you don't know what you're doing, pray to the Father. He loves to help. You'll get his help, and won't be condescended to when you ask for it."
James 1:5

I don't want to give up. I have a request, Lord...

_____

_____

_____

_____

_____

_____

February 28 & 29

2:00 am

"Lynda!" She was crying. "I don't know what to do about my medicine!"

"Mom?"

"Yes, Lynda! It's Mom! There are two bottles on my nightstand and I don't know how they got there! You've got to come over right away!"

"Mom, I'm in Washington. You live in California. I can't get there right away."

"You've got to help me!"

"All right, Mom. Let's do this: Read the label on the first bottle to me, and then count the pills inside. We'll sort this out on the phone, ok?"

"Count the pills? COUNT THE PILLS? (shrieking) I can't count the pills. I don't know how!"

"Tell you what, Mom. I'll catch a plane tomorrow. In the meantime, ask Dad to count the pills for you, OK?"

Oh, Lord, fear has so many faces. And right when I think I've seen them all, I get a big surprise. Help me, God, to respond calmly. Give this one I am caring for a confidence that You are with her – even when she is frightened in the middle of the night. Amen.

THREE

BOOMERS

Love cares more for others than for self.

March 1

"...cares more for others..." "...cares more for others..." That's not a concept that gets tossed around much these days. Usually we hear, "It's dog-eat-dog, you know." "Every man for himself!" "You've got to fight and scratch your way to the top." "If it feels good – do it!" But God said, "Care." And no matter how you spin it – there is no slight of hand or twist of phrase to change its meaning. "Care" means care.

So, what should I do? I could start by replacing this fast-moving, micro-waving, cell-phoning, instant-gratification life with a simpler one. After all, I have to give up some things to make room for this helpless one!

And then I will insert myself into her story. You know, I think I can make a difference!

March 2

My trips to the grocery store have taken on a wonderful senior-citizenly pace, as I now shop with Dad.

"Slow down," he always says. He has been saying that for years. And it never occurred to me that he really meant it! He can't keep up – mentally. As dementia is creeping up on him, he just can't keep up.

My hurry-up pace just isn't for you, is it, Dad?

So, instead of rushing through Safeway, we stroll. Mom takes one cart to set out shopping for the serious items, and Dad and I take a cart of our own. We saunter through the cookie isle, past the Henry's Root Beer, the chocolate ice-cream syrup, and to the bulk candy drawers. I hold open the bag, and Dad fills it. "Annie likes these caramels, doesn't she? We've got to get some chocolates for Bobby. How about the gummy worms for Johnny?" He doesn't remember that our kids no longer live at home. But when they come to visit, he'll sure be ready for 'em!

And the other children! The cranky, crying children in the store. The ones climbing in and out of the shopping carts being pushed by young, overwhelmed moms. He loves talking to those children! And for some strange reason, those Moms allow their little ones to talk to him! He is a crusty ole man with holes in his elbows. He shuffles up to their carts. "Hello," he croons. "How are you today? Are you shopping with your Mommy?" "Cute," he whispers. "So cute."

And rather than bundle up their little ones to protect them from him – the Mommies smile and welcome the brief conversations. For just a moment or two, the little ones stop crying. And Dad has successfully communicated on the only level he knows how.

It must be his eyes. Those endearing eyes. They are the windows to his heart. And even though he cannot express himself well with words, his eyes say "love," "gentleness," "caring."

"You sure do like the grocery story, don't you, Dad?"

"Yeah, you bet."

Cruising Safeway with Dad. What better way to spend a Thursday afternoon?

March 3

Henry and his friend, Justin, had been practicing all week. They had worked out a perfect duet on their saxophones. And the day had finally arrived! They were going with their class to the nursing home, and Henry and Justin would play their number for the residents there.

Henry's Mom was so proud of her little boy. Imagine! Only 10 years old and playing the saxophone! What an accomplishment! And..... he was playing for the old folks. She had been teaching him about caring for the elderly.

As the residents were wheeled into the activity room, little Angela played a piano solo. Then Sammy read a poem. Finally, it was Henry and Justin's turn.

No sooner did they begin their song, *You're a Grand Old Flag*, than an old man in the back of the room began to shout.

"Get me outta here! Help! Get me outta here!"

Henry's mom was livid! Why were they allowing that man to stay in the room? Couldn't the attendants see that he was disrupting the boys?

On the drive home, Mom commented, "I'm sorry about that old man, boys."

"What do you mean, Mom?"

"Well, his rude shouting during your song!"

"Oh, don't worry about that, Mom. He just didn't know what he was doing, that's all. He probably used to be nice."

First surprised. Then softened. Mom had to chuckle at herself.

Out of the mouths of babes!

March 4

The Christian Caregiver

Lawsuits. Boomers are famous for them. We sue everybody about everything. The coffee was too hot. The cigarettes were unhealthy. The baby died.

Many in our generation expect for nothing to go wrong in life, and when it does – they get a lawyer.

As Christian caregivers, we have a different worldview. We move about in a world embroiled in suffering. And we don't plan lawsuits. We help out.

March 5

He changed his clothes five times. He was so excited! A jazz saxophonist his whole life, Bob hadn't been invited to play recently; not since his dementia became so obvious. But this was going to be a big party! And there would be other musicians there!

Making a final decision on the duds, he was ready to go. "So, who's the band?"

"Well, Dad, there's not really a band. Just a guitar player. And he's got one of those background machines that plays bass and drums."

"Oh, I see. So, where's this band from?"

"He's from California. It's just one guy, Dad. It just a little birthday party for my friend."

"Oh. California, huh? They have good bands in California."

"Yeah, Dad, they do."

Upon their arrival, his son put the sax together, accompanied him onto the stage, and hung it around Bob's neck.

The 'band' started playing "Girl From Ipanema", his son began singing the words and melody into his ear, and Bob started to blow. He was making music again!

Whenever he got lost in the song, his son would sing a little louder, and Bob would remember where he was.

He left the stage to resounding applause. The joy in his eyes flowed into the crowd. He was lovin' it!

On the way home, father and son reveled in the accomplishment. "So, Dad, how did it feel to be up there on stage again?"

"It was great! But you know, that kid? That guitar player?"

"Yeah, Dad?"

"He couldn't even keep up with me!"

March 6

See life with His perspective.
Seize life with His power.

Know what? I need to correct my thinking! Especially about...

_____

_____

_____

_____

_____

_____

March 7

Hospital

Aw, Dad, I know you're in tremendous pain. That was a bad fall you took. I know that you are afraid, too. But, I can't see the 'guys' you're talking about. If I could, I would chase them away for you. It's just us in this room. We're at the hospital.

No, I don't see the wires on your hands. Well, Ok, you can hand them to me. I'll get rid of them.

Nurse! Please bring a sedative!

It's going to get better, Dad. We're gonna get you fixed up. Then we'll go back home together, ok?

No, there are no other guys in the room.

Nurse!

Oh, God, please help my Dad. Please take away this delirium.

It's x-ray time now, Dad. Yes, I'll be here when you get

back. In fact, I will come with you, ok? Everything is going
to be all right.

I promise I won't leave you alone.

*Boy, Lord, don't I sound like the brave one? I am
shaking in my boots! Give me confidence in this
time of emergency, God.*

March 8

Though your duty may be hard
Look not on it as an ill;
If it be an honest task
Do it with an honest will. *Unknown*

*"But because God was so gracious, so very gener-
ous, here I am. And I'm not about to let his grace
go to waste." 1 Corinthians 15:10*

March 9

She was a different type of nursing home resident. Her
mind was all there. Her body just didn't cooperate anymore.
She had had a stroke, due to her 40 years of smoking
cigarettes, which disabled the right side of her body.

She had the electric kind of wheelchair, so she could get
around on her own – including trips to the garden area where
she could smoke.

Bernice told us that she had previously been in the state-
run home right after her stroke –"not nearly as nice as this
one" – and that her son had arranged for this cleaner, private
facility. "Just for awhile, though. He's going to take me
home with him, soon." She looked forward to that day.

In the meantime, Bernice wrote poetry. Gripping poetry. Her mind was keen, indeed. Each time we came to do a church service, she would patiently wait, holding her notebook on her lap, until we invited her to read a selection. We so enjoyed listening to her.

Then came the time when Bernice did not show up at the service. We were happy for her!

"Her son came to get her?" Rejoicing.

"Oh, no! She ran out of money. She moved over to the state facility. Her son is just too busy to take care of her right now. Besides, he doesn't like her smoking."

March 10

Every Sunday they make a choice. They come to a "Y" in the road. They can veer off to the left where they will eventually come to the Little League field, or turn right to wind up a little hill to the parking lot of the church.

"Which is more fun?" they ask themselves. For more and more families the Little League wins out – hands down. And why not? After all, it's healthy, vigorous, family-oriented. It teaches good sportsmanship, fair play, and teamwork. You find people up there who are dedicated and hard working. Little League is a good thing!

And what happens up there at the church? Well...there are dedicated and hard-working people there, too. The activities there are healthy, vigorous, totally family-oriented. But sometimes they don't have so much fun. You see, they have to deal with 'broken' people.

That's what you have decided to do, Caregiver. You've decided to help the broken ones. You're probably not having a lot of fun. But take heart!

The Awards Banquet will be a blast!

March 11

I've wrestled with reality for 35 years, and I'm glad to say I've finally won out over it. *Jimmy Stewart in the movie, "Harvey"*

"Life's a lot easier now that I am in denial."

"I don't have to notice Mom's problems: the bad hygiene, the dirty house, the unpaid bills, the word salad. All the signs of Alzheimer's disease."

"I have always been quite good at compartmentalizing my life. It makes it more convenient when I don't have to combine issues. Like, my Christian walk – I do not have to put it up against my business life, right? They are in different compartments. The same goes for the Alzheimer's. This way, I can still go to church and not have to worry about blending that part of my life with my other decisions."

Sound crazy? Do you know how many people in our generation live and think that way?

I praise God for you, Caregiver. You are the genuine article.

"Every time I think of you – and I think of you often! – I thank God for your lives of free and open access to God, given by Jesus. There's no end to what has happened in you – it's beyond speech, beyond knowledge. The evidence of Christ has been clearly verified in your [life]." 1 Corinthians 1:4-6

March 12

If thy heart be like my heart, then give me thine hand. *John Wesley*

I am so blessed by those who help me in my work...

_____

_____

_____

_____

_____

_____

March 13

Claire and her siblings agreed. They would put Mom in a nursing home. She would be 'better off.' They would visit often. They would take her out for the chocolate malted shakes that she liked so much.

That way, they could get on with their lives. I mean, Mom always said that she didn't want to be a burden. All three kids had careers, families, and community responsibilities. Two of them lived clear on the other side of the country! Yes, this was the solution. They had it all figured out.

But there was one element to this that hadn't occurred to Claire. She never would have imagined that Mom wouldn't like her life in an institution! During her visits, she heard constant complaining: the food was no good; her room was too small; the aides didn't know what they were doing. After the first few weeks, she even asked if Claire would take her home. Claire asked her to just try it for a while more.

It got worse and worse with each visit, until Claire's mom was begging to get out, and Claire did not know what to do.

Soon, Claire had had enough, and she stopped visiting her mom. She reasoned that her visits were not good for her mother – the begging was evidence of that. "Besides, Mom probably doesn't even remember that I visited."

You know someone like that, don't you? The little lady who no one visits anymore? The old man who spends Father's Day alone? The ones whose kids don't think it important to honor their parents once they become infirmed.

Caregiver, you play an important role here. You are the friendly face. You provide the gentle touch that each one needs so much. You give the hugs.

God bless you as you try to fill the shoes of loved ones who are missing.

March 14

"I'd do anything for you."

"I'd do anything for *you*."

Easy to say. Tougher to do.

They had been best friends for years. So many years, they had lost count.

Went to school together. Went to church together. Laughed together. Wept together.

They held each other up through the deaths of their parents. Divorce. Broken homes. Broken hearts.

"I'm always here for you!"

Then Rosie got sick. "Kind of like Leukemia", she told Liz. The doctors gave her 5% chance if she didn't get the bone marrow transplant. 30% chance if she did.

Her children were grown and lived far away. Her husband left when the going got tough. She had just buried her mom. She was all alone.

"Liz, the doctor says I have to have someone take care of me 24/7 while I go through this. I'll be very ill. I'll be weak. Throwing up. Very, very sick. And I might not make it. I could die at any time. Will you take me in?"

Inside, Liz was screaming. She hated herself for her own feelings. This would mean giving up her vacation plans. "I actually thought about *myself* and how this would tie me down!"

Everybody feels that way – even caregivers. We are all selfish. In fact, we are *obsessed* with ourselves! The trick is in getting over it and doing the right thing.

When we practice *doing* the right things – eventually our hearts catch up.

March 15

Margaret was a lady through and through. It showed especially at dinnertime. When all of the other nursing home residents would hobble down to dinner in their bathrobes or 'whatever,' Margaret did just the opposite. She dressed to the nines.

One evening, she attempted to look particularly appealing. She wore a lovely navy and white polka-dot dress, cute hat, and matching bag and shoes. For she was interested in Mr. Ray Tomkin, a dapper old gentleman who had just moved into Deer Haven Nursing Home.

She made her way down the long hallway to the dining room. As she spotted Mr. Tomkin, she picked up her step, hoping to eventually catch up with him.

Out of the blue, a small, bent-over woman grabbed her by the arm. Margaret gently pulled her arm away. The woman took hold again. "Let go," Margaret quietly demanded. Nope. Still holding tight.

A nurse, witnessing the event, came to the rescue. "C'mon, Georgette, let's walk over this way," taking the old woman to the nurse's station. "You can visit with me."

Just then, red light flashing, the nurse was called to another room. Forced to leave Georgette alone for a minute, she said, "Dear, why don't you just hold this counter edge until I return?"

But, of course, a moving target is more fun than an idle one. As quickly as she could, Georgette caught up with Margaret, who was, coincidentally, just catching up with Mr. Tomkin. She once again grabbed her arm.

"Let go," whispered Margaret in her usual lady-like manner. "Please let go."

No response.

"Look, lady!" Margaret then bellowed. "Let go or I'll deck ya!"

March 16

Do all the good you can,
By all the means you can,
In all the ways you can,
In all the places you can,
To all the people you can,
As long as ever you can. *John Wesley*

March 17

God's grace exalts a man without inflating him and humbles a man without degrading him. *Adrian Rogers*

"So this is my prayer: that your love will flourish and that you will not only love much but well. Learn to love appropriately. You need to use your head and test your feelings so that your love is sincere and intelligent, not sentimental gush. Live a lover's life, circumspect and exemplary, a life Jesus will be proud of: bountiful in fruits from the soul, making Jesus Christ attractive to all, getting everyone involved in the glory and praise

of God." Philippians 1:9-11

March 18

When the Scotsman shivers
Beneath his kilts
He'll run to the closet
For Grandma's quilts. (*old road sign in Montana*)

how 'bout...
Within this vale
Of toil and sin
Your head grows bald
But not your chin. (*Burma Shave*)

Go ahead, Boomer. You can laugh. The simpler humor of the 'old days' is refreshing!

I praise You, God, for this old one I care for. Help *me* to simplify by...

_____

_____

_____

_____

_____

_____

March 19

Click Click. Car door's open.

Rolling through Starbuck's, "I'll have a grande non-fat caramel machiato, please."

Now it's off to the cleaners to pick up our clothes – drive

through, of course.

Next the drive-through at the pharmacy, the drive-through at the bank, a quick trip through McDonald's for lunch.

What's next? Drive-through Communion?

(There's a whole community of people, you know, who cannot keep up in this hurry-up world.)

March 20
First Day of Spring

Maybe being an artist that the world calls an artist is a feature I don't have, but I'm going to paint a picture.

Maybe being a musician that the world calls a musician is a feature I don't have, but I'm going to sing a song.

And maybe being a dancer that the worlds calls a dancer is a feature I don't have, but I'm going to dance until sunset.

'Cause, hey! It's springtime!

"Look around you: Winter is over; the winter rains are over, gone!" Song of Songs 2:11

March 21

It was one of 'those' days at the nursing home. The kind that makes you wonder why you even bother visiting.

As soon as we walked through the door it hit us in the face: a strong, obnoxious odor. It was awful!

I no sooner put my bag down so I could shake some hands when a lady grabbed my arm and would not let go. I patted her, smiled, talked to her, and tried to escape, but no, it wasn't working. An aide came to my rescue.

We got set up – turned on the music – and a resident yelled from the back of the room, "That's too loud! What are you trying to do to us? Turn that music down!" Another person who couldn't hear well complained that the music was not loud enough!

We made some adjustments and continued: We sang a song – sort of upbeat – and then a hymn, something for everybody. Some folks clapped along, some slumped over – sound asleep.

I read an uplifting verse from the Bible and said, "Let's pray."

"Pray?" we heard a screech from the little lady right up front. "What do you mean, pray? What the blankety-blank are you guys doin' here, anyway?"

Once again, an aide came to the rescue and wheeled the angry one out of the room – we could hear her cussing all the way down the hall.

I determined that we would hurry up and get this over with – some weeks things just don't go well – when I noticed Connie, a sweet-faced lady in the back of the room.

She was trying to say something, but speaking so softly I couldn't hear her. I thought she was making a song request, so I approached her.

"I, I, I, I, I, I, I, I, ..." Voice fading out.

"LO, LO, LO, LO, LO, LO, LOVE...."

"Y, Y, Y, Y, YOU...."

I LOVE YOU! She was saying, "I love you!"

I took Connie's hand. I told her I loved her, too.

We finished up by singing a couple more hymns, and to my amazement Connie's words came through loud and clear. Her love for those songs won out over the speech impediment!

In the weeks to come, I looked to Connie often – to encourage her and to be encouraged. Then came a day when Connie no longer joined us for 'church.' She had gone to be with her Lord.

Each time we visit now, I pause to search the room for a

special one. Someone who loves and needs to be loved back. It's easy to miss them when you're in a hurry.

March 22

As I pulled onto the freeway off 65th Street I cringed, noticing that it was five o'clock. Peak-hour traffic was the last thing I wanted to face. The cars zoomed by me, and my left-hand signal and I fought to move over one lane into the traffic. Cars zigzagged in and out of the lanes trying to move maybe one car length ahead and just a little bit faster than anybody else.

The whole scene reminded me of the supermarket. People with shopping carts, kids running, jumping, screaming. Look out, lady, I'm cutting over to the meat section. Uh oh – there seems to be some hang-up a few feet ahead. Collision! The lady in the raincoat/the'72 Corvette ran into the bakery counter/the blue SUV. Nobody hurt? O.K. Keep moving. You're blocking traffic.

Now it's one, two, three, and hit the checkout stand! Traffic surged to the left, pushing, shoving. Who can get out first? Please! Don't crowd. Don't shove. There's plenty of room for everybody!

And as I rage about those who rush by me, I must stop to consider: Who did I push by or shove out of the way today?

"Step out of the traffic! Take a long, loving look at me, your High God..." Psalm 46:10

March 23

"She hit me!" the old lady yelled out. "That girl hit me!"

"I just shooked her hand," cried four-year-old Taylor. "I held her hand."

The lady continued screaming all the way down the hall as the aide removed her from our little church service. Little Taylor trembled and cried.

Bad experience at the nursing home. We were doing our best, but it went sour.

Does that sound familiar to you, Caregiver?

Oh, Lord, bless those who are insulted, yelled at, and maligned in the course of duty as Helpers to the Helpless. Keep them going, God. Amen.

March 24

Far and away the best prize that life offers is the chance to work hard at work worth doing. *Theodore Roosevelt*

God, please help me to slow down enough to figure out what is important.

My priorities are...

_____

_____

_____

_____

_____

_____

March 25

"Are you ready to meet your Maker?"

That's how they used to ask the question. Back when folks weren't so 'sensitive.'

That's what I like about the Greatest Generation. They are forthright. They say what they mean and mean what they say.

We Boomers are different. We use words that tickle the ears – symbolism over substance. Because, after all, truth is relative, isn't it? My truth is not your truth and your truth is not my truth. So let's just hold hands and sing *Kumbayah*. We've learned to avoid confrontation by not holding anyone accountable.

But there will come a day, when no matter which generation is doing the talking, there will be an **unavoidable accounting**.

And that's when we all had better be ready to 'Meet Our Maker.'

(We really should listen more to our elders.)

March 26

A lot has changed over the years. But Christianity hasn't.

New life means new motivation. We still have to make three conscious commitments:

1. Lordship of Christ
2. Body of Christ
3. Work of Christ

March 27

"There's an opportune time to do things, a right time for everything on the earth:

A right time for birth and another for death,
A right time to plant and another to reap,
A right time to kill and another to heal,

A right time to destroy and another to construct,
A right time to cry and another to laugh,
A right time to lament and another to cheer,
A right time to make love and another to abstain,
A right time to embrace and another to part,
A right time to search and another to count your losses,
A right time to hold on and another to let go,
A right time to rip out and another to mend,
A right time to shut up and another to speak up,
A right time to love and another to hate,
A right time to wage war and another to make peace."
Ecclesiastes 3:1-8

Whoa, Boomer! There is a speed limit! You can't do everything at once!

March 28

"I would like to have what you all have, faith in God. But I just don't think I'm good enough to get to heaven."

"I try to do good things. I'm nice to people. I try to be friends with the people who I know are righteous."

"I feel guilty. I wish I hadn't..."

"I'm doing my best. I am the caregiver for my wife. That must count for something!"

Oh, Lord, how do I get through to him? How do I convince him that You are too rich to sell salvation and we are too poor to buy it?

March 29

Believe in something larger than yourself. *Barbara Bush*

"Mr. and Mrs. Jones, let me begin by saying that I consider your keeping your mother at home has been nothing short of an heroic effort."

"Heroic effort?"

"Hmmmyes, but I do think you need to consider now the possibility of putting her into some sort of professional care."

"But, Doctor, that would only frighten her. And we promised Mom we would take care of her when we first found out that she has Alzheimer's disease."

"Surely it is a good idea to keep her as long as she is able to enjoy your company and you can enjoy hers, but she really doesn't know who you are anymore." (shuffling through the file) "It says here that she does not respond to the mention of your names and that her cognitive skills are virtually gone."

"But, Doctor, have you looked into her eyes?"

Lord, although the conversations don't happen anymore, remind me to look into her eyes. She needs me, God, and I need her. Caring for her allows me to live and believe beyond myself. Amen.

March 30

"Summing up: Be agreeable, be sympathetic, be loving, be compassionate, be humble." 1 Peter 3:8

I want to be like You, Jesus. I will try harder when...

_____

_____

_____

_____

_____

March 31

Folk Medicine. Some of it seems so ridiculous to us 'sophisticated' ones.

Take the mustard plaster, for example. My mother always put one on me if I had a high fever and bad chest congestion. How strange is that?

Grandpa used to give us a tablespoon of cod liver oil with turpentine in it for a cold! *Turpentine*!

Ever try to drink water with your head upside-down for hiccups? How about putting a bag over your head?

A mudpack on a bee sting?

"Early to bed – early to rise – makes a man healthy and wealthy and wise."

"An apple a day keeps the doctor away."

Now wait a minute! I just heard something on the news the other day about apples.

And Chicken Soup? They are discovering good stuff about that, too!

Hmmmmm.... Maybe we shouldn't be so quick to ridicule our elders.

Instead, we should pull up a chair! Listen to their stories! Honor them with our attention. Glean the nuggets of wisdom that are undeniably there.

Heavens to Betsy, Boomers! Let's not throw out the baby with the bath water!

FOUR

THE BUCK $ STOPS HERE

Love doesn't want what it doesn't have.

April 1

Oh, Beloved Caregiver,

When you took on the care of this infirmed one, it probably did not occur to you that you might have to worry about things like monthly bills, writing wills, Medicaid, Medicare, secondary insurance, and all other money matters. Sometimes you are asked to handle these things for the infirmed. Sometimes they still want to do it themselves, and you watch them struggle trying to manage it.

Part of the job is discerning when to step in and when to just let things be.

The solution is always in the heart:

Jump in only when it's good for **somebody else** that you do so.

April 2

Whenever I have money, I give it away quickly lest it burn a hole in my heart. *John Wesley*

April 3

"So, Mrs. Smith, your daughter has asked that I notarize the documents here on my desk. Let's see here, we have a Durable Power of Attorney for Health Care. Now, do you understand, Ma'am, what this document says?"

"Yes," said Mom. "I believe I do."

"Can you explain it to me?"

Mom looked at me for the right words.

I said, "Well, it says that if something should happen to Mom and she cannot make proper decisions about her health care, then I can answer on her behalf."

The Notary Public did not acknowledge that I had spoken. She continued to look at Mom for the answer. Mom saw that the woman was waiting for her to speak, so she repeated what I said.

"Now, are you signing this document free-willing with no coercion of any kind?" *NOW* she looked at me.

"Why, yes, of course," answered my mother.

"Very well." She handed over the papers for Mom and me to sign.

This lady fancied herself to be my mother's advocate. And in the process of her questioning, I first felt humiliated and then enraged at the thought that I was somehow under suspicion. Suspicion for what? For having Mom fill out these papers? What possible benefit was there in it for me? It is tough to make decisions for somebody else concerning their health.

Dear Caregiver, if you are in the same position; if you are required to take responsibility for your parents' health decisions – do not feel bad about it! Because you love your mom or dad and only want what's best for them – you are the *real* advocate. You hold the noble position.

April 4

Grandma took care of me every weekend while Mom and Dad worked. She was my "weekend caregiver." Of course, my parents could not afford to pay her, but she was happy to have me stay with her in her little apartment.

She earned her living by scrubbing floors. Grandpa had died young, and Social Security did not pay all the bills, so Grandma went to work doing what she knew how to do.

She cleaned the local grade school every evening: cleaning bathrooms, mopping hallways, washing off the desktops. Sometimes she let me wipe the chalkboards!

I never heard Grandma complain about money. She would not have dreamed of asking for a handout. She gave regularly to her church and delighted in giving gifts to us grandkids.

She was grateful for what God had provided. She never wanted what she did not have. She was the happiest person I knew.

Lord, I know that as a caregiver, I'm not going to strike it rich. Help me to be content with that.

April 5

I stay close to my own heart, listening carefully to what I have heard and felt. I also stay close to the hearts of those whose joys and pains are touching me most at this time of my life. Most of all, I stay close to the heart of Jesus, whose life and death are the main source for understanding and living my own life and death. *Henri J.M. Nouwen* [5]

April 6

I'm happy with God receiving the glory as long as I get the credit!

Oh, Lord, I have a confession...

_____

_____

_____

_____

_____

April 7

We are to love people and use things –
Rather than love things and use people.

April 8

The Sermon on the Amount

Abby had acquired Power of Attorney for her mother years ago – back when Mom could think straight. Since then, Abby had made frequent trips to the assisted living apartment where her mother lived.

She would straighten things up, talk her mom into getting a shower, take her out to dinner and maybe a movie. She helped out several times each week.

Mom had money to pay her own expenses from Social Security and some stocks and bonds. So when Abby found a bankbook showing $80,000 in savings, she didn't think twice about cashing it in. *Mom will never need this*, she thought to herself. *And I am her only heir!*

She and her husband went to Mexico. Then Hawaii. Abby bought all new furniture. They bought their son a new car and gave their daughter money for a down payment on a new home. The grandkids fared very well, too.

When her mom died, Abby discovered that Mom had intended to leave a large sum of money to her church. According to the will, it was to come out of the $80,000!

Grave Error – Exposure – Humiliation

Oh, Lord! Give us discernment about how much pay we should receive for our care-giving duties. Keep us from getting greedy. Put a hedge of protection around us, Father, before we get ourselves into trouble. Amen.

April 9

THE LONG AND THE SHORT OF IT IS –
SOMETIMES YOU JUST GOT TO OUTWIT 'EM.

She knew her dad was dangerous on the roads now. He just had to stop driving.

After all, he was 92 years old! His mind was losing its sharpness, and his physical capabilities were just not up to snuff.

She had mentioned it to her dad several times, only to get a very strong reaction! But then, what did she expect? Taking away the car was like taking away what little independence he had left. He was already having trouble handling his money by himself. It was getting harder and harder to read – presbyopia, you know. And now this.

She shared her concerns with her sweet, little mother. Her darling mama - you know – the one with the halo on?

And, boy, did Mom surprise her! Realizing what was at stake, she did what any submissive and loving wife would do.

She found the title to the car. She carefully placed a piece of paper over the title, with the exception of the line where the seller signs when selling the car. She then took it to her husband, told him it was a random form that they had to sign for their landlord. He signed it – no questions asked.

"Mom! You lied to Dad!"

She handed the title over to her daughter and whispered, "Don't worry, Honey. God will forgive me for loving your dad this much."

April 10

Leah had been caring for her Aunt Norma for about twenty-five years. Her own mother had died at an early age, and Leah considered she was honoring her aunt by tending to her care-giving. Norma had no children.

Serving as the Principal in a small Christian school, Leah had no retirement plan – except to trust in Jesus for her old age. She mentioned to Aunt Norma time and time again through the years that she should probably work in the public schools, so that she could put away some money.

And time and time again, Aunt Norma argued, saying that she would 'take care' of Leah when it was time for her to retire.

At 92, Norma died, leaving behind an estate in the neighborhood of $700,000. To everyone's amazement, the bulk of the money had been left to a Christian university, with a small portion going to Leah.

At first hurt, and then suspicious, Leah investigated. A university procurement lawyer had visited with Aunt Norma two times in the past year. (Norma had taken classes at that school 70 years prior.) During the visits, the lawyer drew up new wills for Norma, naming the university as the prime beneficiary.

Leah complained – to no avail. She hired an attorney, who contested the will, explaining to the Christian university's lawyers that they were dealing with the Principal of a little Christian school who had no retirement benefit.

The response? "We'll win in court, because we had Norma sign two different wills, six months apart. In your state, you cannot contest two wills."

So, while everyone fumed – friends, co-workers, church members, and lawyers – the only one in the situation who remained calm was Leah. She was still trusting in

Jesus for her future.

~~~

Praising God for what we *have* – prevents pride and promotes perspective.

April 11

REMEMBER!

"This is how much God loved the world: He gave his Son, his one and only Son. And this is why: so that no one need be destroyed; by believing in him, anyone can have a whole and lasting life. God didn't go to all the trouble of sending his Son merely to point an accusing finger, telling the world how bad it was. He came to help, to put the world right again." John 3:16-17

April 12

You cannot tell a true Christian by how he acts, but rather, how he reacts.

Ouch!

Lord, when things go wrong, I pray that...

_____

_____

_____

_____

_____

_____

April 13

He can't read anymore. He fakes it at the restaurants now. He looks at the menu, and then asks the waitress, "What'd ya recommend?" "Great! I'll take that!"

He struggles with numbers – the man who developed the entire parts-numbering system for a Naval shipyard cannot discern between $100 and $100,000.

He sits with his calculator every day, trying to refigure his finances. He can't remember how much money he has anymore.

He said he wanted to sell his house; he wanted to get at least "100 bucks" for it.

Yesterday he handed me the phone while he was talking to his insurance agent. He could not understand what she was saying to him. He had defeat in his eyes as he asked me to "finish up" talking to her.

Managing his stuff is overwhelming for him now. His eyes are so sad.

That's why I stepped in.

April 14

If God is your Co-Pilot, swap seats!

"And now to him who can keep you on your feet, standing tall in his bright presence, fresh and celebrating – to our one God, our only Savior, through Jesus Christ, our Master, be glory, majesty, strength, and rule before all time, and now, and to the end of all time. Yes." Jude 24

April 15

Lucille wanted to sell her house for way too much money. It was true that it was a waterfront property. She did have a little deli/store and a dock on the water. It was a valuable piece of real estate. But she was asking an unreasonable price.

Unreasonable to anybody who didn't see the whole picture, that is. For Lucille was not only selling her little business and her home, she was selling her memories. She had been on that property even before she married her beloved husband, Leander. They had had a wonderful life together there. And after he died, she held on to that place very tightly, as if letting go would erase all those years with him.

So Lucille put a big price tag on it, even though she was dying.

A friend tried talking sense into her; telling her that it couldn't possibly sell for that high price! And, besides that, she shouldn't be so 'married' to a piece of property. Wasn't she a Christian?

So many people cling to their belongings as they grow old. Even Christians. More often than not, the hanging on to the world is just a symptom of fear.

Understand it, Caregiver. Soothe the dying one. This isn't the time to major in minors. After she's gone, the 'stuff' can be taken care of.

For now, just be there for her. Read a Scripture. Sing a song. Recall a pleasant memory. Stroke her forehead. Make her comfortable.

Make sure her loved ones are aware. Call Hospice.

The House? The Money? Non-issues.

April 16

Promises never take the place of performance.

O God, please keep me from making promises that I cannot keep. Amen.

April 17

Lord, is it time to take over her finances? She forgot to pay her rent. She ordered the same magazine two times. Then she wrote three checks that she forgot to enter in the checkbook – all in one day!

Give me a gentle spirit, God, so that I will not insult her when I suggest the take-over of her money matters. Please don't let her get embarrassed.

April 18

Why is the Dead Sea dead?
Because it only receives – it never gives.

Lord, I have needs! But so does this one I am caring for! Help me to...

_____
_____
_____
_____
_____
_____

April 19

David and Sarah had worked hard. Just a few years short of retirement, their investments were doing well and they were looking forward to their golden years of travel and good living. They had about $500,000 in their portfolio and would be millionaires by the time they were finished. They were banking on that.

Then, the corporate scandals. In the twinkling of an eye it was all gone! They were back at first base. Of course, they were crushed. They would never get over the anger.

This is what the world offers.

Jesus had a different idea:

"Don't hoard treasure down here where it gets eaten by moths and corroded by rust or – worse! – stolen by burglars. Stockpile treasure in heaven, where it's safe from moth and rust and burglars. It's obvious, isn't it? The place where your treasure is, is the place you will most want to be, and end up being." Matthew 6:19-21

It's OK to have stuff. But don't bet your future on it!

April 20

Lynda had come to check Mom out of the hospital, and decided it was a good idea to get her mother's paperwork in order – just in case there was another, more serious stroke.

As Lynda and her mom sat at the Notary Public's desk, filling out the forms for Power of Attorney, the Notary kept interrupting:

"Now, Mrs. Gadsby, do you understand what you just put on that form? You just gave your daughter the right to write checks from your account. Is that what you want?" Looking smug.

"Why, yes, I think so," answered Mom, looking over at Lynda to see if that answer was ok.

"And you realize that your daughter can now draw money from your bank account?" Again, looking at Lynda suspiciously.

Finally, feeling accused, Lynda said, "Ya know what? I think Mom and I will finish this up over lunch. C'mon, Mom, let's go have a bite to eat."

She had had enough of this Notary. Lynda fully understood that the job of Notary Public is to verify that the person who is signing is who they say they are – with a show of identification or some other means of proving who they are. Sometimes a Notary may have to question whether the person is mentally competent or not, but this was getting down right insulting!

So Lynda and her mom went to a cozy restaurant to go through the remaining questions on the Power of Attorney form. They thoroughly discussed each item, and her mother was agreeable to the whole idea of Lynda making financial decisions for her in case she could not.

So now, a bit frazzled, but feeling that the job was well done, Lynda took her mom to the local bank to find a Notary Public – hopefully a friendlier one.

The new Notary looked over the papers, and said to Lynda's mom, "You understand all this stuff?"

"What stuff?" Mom asked.

AHHHHG!!!!!!!

April 21

This is not our reigning time – it's our training time!

April 22

Fiduciaries = Trustees (emphasis on the TRUST)

Now you've gotten the Power of Attorney like everyone told you to do. Now you can sign the legal papers concerning money. And now your parent wants for you to pay the bills, work with Medicare, and keep track of the money. "I can still do it," says Mom. I just don't *want* to." But, really? She just cannot keep up with it. She is vulnerable.

You've had a good look at her financial situation, talked with her about this account and that account, and you've discovered that your mom is very nervous about all things regarding money.

What every caregiver has to promise to do is not spend another's money frivolously. And then, KEEP THE PROMISE!

You need God's heart and mind to pull it off.

"Don't become so well-adjusted to your culture that you fit into it without even thinking. Instead, fix your attention on God. You'll be changed from the inside out. Readily recognize what he wants from you, and quickly respond to it. Unlike the culture around you, always dragging you down to its level of immaturity, God brings the best out of you, develops well-formed maturity in you." Romans 12:2

April 23

About my thought – treat it gently – it's in a strange place. *Grandma Garrity*

Lord, I'm not a brainiac. The job of taking care of

my parents' money is certainly a test for me. You know, I've not been real good with my own money, and now I am handling theirs! Keep my heart in a good place. Help me to do a good job. Thank you, God, for giving me clear thinking about this. Amen.

April 24

A lot of kneeling will keep you in good standing.
I offer this prayer today...

_____

_____

_____

_____

_____

_____

April 25

Sandie's dad kept escaping from his Alzheimer's wing. But they were ready for him. The nurses on the ward kept track of him through a little electronic device wrapped around his ankle. If he got out of bed in the middle of the night – they knew it. When he wandered outside – he was caught in the act.

He did not say much anymore, but occasionally showed great concern about his finances. He would mumble to anyone within hearing distance, "How about my bills?" "Is my money OK?"

One day, he asked his nurse, "What's going on with my money?"

She was wise. "See that thing on your ankle Mr.

McCurdy?"

"Yes."

"That thing means you're all paid up."

He could now relax.

Lord, give me the right words when this infirmed one needs an answer. Words that will calm his heart.

April 26

Now that Dad is in the nursing home, we should probably buy him some things.

Like what?

Well, we can get a new car so that we can take him out for dinner and stuff and he'll be comfortable.

Yeah?

And we should get all the rest we can – maybe take a vacation – so that we will have the energy to take better care of him when we get back.

Yeah?

And if we buy that condo at the beach, then we'll have a great place to bring him every year!

Is that what Dad wants done with his money? I mean, he loves God so much. Don't you think he might want for *some* of it to go to the church?

Look! He gave his whole life to the church. I think it's time for the family now. I'm sure he wants his money to be a **blessing** for **us**!

(Well, would you look at that? The devil got all dressed up today!)

April 27

Did you know that there are two American Dreams? There always have been.

Long ago when the Mayflower set out for America, there were two types of idealists on board: the Pilgrims, who came for freedom to worship God the way they wanted to, and the Merchant Adventurers, who came seeking financial gain.

All were brave souls, facing hardships we can hardly imagine. But they differed in what they thought was important.

It's much the same today. Some are climbing the corporate ladder, working their way toward financial triumph. Others seek God's kingdom first, and consider success a new soul for that kingdom.

Make no mistake about it – the two require different lifestyles.

We'd like to believe that we can entertain both dreams, but remember this:

> *"You can't worship two gods at once. Loving one god, you'll end up hating the other. Adoration of one feeds contempt for the other. You can't worship God and Money both." Matthew 6:24*

April 28

Remember – you haven't inherited it yet!

April 29

"Yes, Social Security office? My name is Laurie Zurinsky and I am calling on behalf of my dad."

"Is your father with you now?"

"Yes, he's right here."

"Will you put him on? I need to verify that you may speak for him."

"Ummm," (whispering) "He has dementia and doesn't converse well. I just want to notify you that Dad lives with us now and wants his checks deposited into his local bank here. I have Power of Attorney for him. I do all his paperwork."

"I'm sorry, but I cannot make any changes until I speak with him."

"Ok then." (*You asked for it*, I thought) "I'll put him on... Dad, this gentleman wants to ask you a couple of questions so that he knows I can speak for you."

"Hello?"

"Mr. Mickelson?"

"Yes?"

"I just need to ask you a couple of questions to verify that you are who you say you are."

"Oh?"

"Yes sir, can you give me your social security number?"

"Uh, you'll have to ask my daughter about that."

"Well, how about your birth date?"

No answer.

"OK. Well, perhaps you can give me your mother's maiden name."

(I whisper in Dad's ear, "Smet.")

"I heard that!" said the Social Security guy. (oops!)

"Let's see......how about your middle name?"

(Whispering softer this time, "Emmet.")

"Emmet."

"Oh! Very good! OK, Mr. Mickelson, what color are your eyes?"

(What color are his eyes? How could the Social Security guy possibly know the answer?) I wrote on a piece of paper – "Blue."

"Blue."

"Oh, very good, Mr. Mickelson. OK, you can put your daughter back on."

Oh, Lord, thank You for letting me get hold of the kindest Social Security worker in the whole Administration.

April 30

Love that reaches up is adoration.
Love that reaches across is affection.
Love that reaches down is grace. *Barnhouse*

Jesus, You reached down for me. And for this infirmed one, too! I offer You this praise...

_____

_____

_____

_____

_____

_____

FIVE

GIMME A BREAK

Love doesn't strut,
Doesn't have a swelled head.

May 1

Whew! I'm beat. This is a lot of work! And here I thought I could handle this on my own.

I guess there was a certain amount of arrogance that went along with my decision to enter into this work. Thinking that I could handle the physical and emotional stress all by myself.

I've stretched myself to the limit, but there is a glimmer of hope. I finally realize that I am not superhuman. (Go figure!) Now I'm ready and willing to listen to anybody who has been here, done this, and earned the t-shirt. I need to be part of a community! A care-giving community.

The response to my outcry has been overwhelming! I am amazed at how kind other caregivers are – they *want* to come alongside me! All I had to do was ask!

It's so nice to hear someone say, "No matter how bad it gets, I am with you. You are not alone."

May 2

The "Do-It-Yourself" doctrine is not found in Scripture.
Selected

Kathy had been taking care of her dad for a couple of years. He suffered from dementia, and sometimes the job was overwhelming! She felt quite alone in her task, until she confided in her friend, Sharon, about her insecurities.

Sharon had been caring for her stepmother who was suffering from Parkinson's disease. Sharon had big shoulders, and Kathy enjoyed their talks immensely. And she learned a lot, too!

Cher's mom had a stroke. When the job got too big for her, she knew she could call on Kathy for support.

Later, Felicia's mom became gravely ill, requiring a full-time caregiver. She had heard about Cher, and gave her a call.

And the beat goes on....

Oh, Caregiver! It is so important! Get connected.

May 3

What does your giant look like, Caregiver? That thing that keeps you awake at night? We all have one: the problem that won't go away; the discomfort that you want to avoid? But you won't run away for long, right?

Because a person of faith looks the giant in the face and attacks! You must know that if God is with you, your giant just became a wimp!

Face him. Even embrace him. And then kick him in the knee.

May 4

Do your best and then sleep in peace. God is awake.

May 5

"Sheets and pillowcases!" she would say when she got mad. And if she was really boiling over, it was, "Feather beds!"

Always the lady. Full of spunk, but never crass.

Until she was overcome by stroke. Then her whole personality changed. The "sheets and pillowcases" gave way to profanities. "Sounds like @#%#$# to me!" she would complain loudly. Even in front of the children! Mom was just not herself anymore.

Dottie kept her mom with her – just for a while, " 'til she feels better."

Her mom's attitude changed; she became fearful. Dottie asked her to stay on awhile longer, so she could "keep her safe and sound."

One day, Dottie held her mom's arm – helping her walk to her favorite chair. Mom paused in the middle of the room.

"Let's keep going, Mom," Dottie urged.

"I would if I could," said her mom. She never walked again, so Dottie bought a wheelchair.

Soon, Mom needed to stay in bed most of the time. Dottie cared for her needs day and night until the day she died.

When looking at options for caring for my dad, Dottie said, "Just keep him with you. It will just be a little while, and you will never regret it."

And I never did.

Who do *you* listen to? It's really important.

May 6

If you can't get over that hurdle – step back and get a longer run at it. *Dottie Bell*

Good advice from one who has been there! When I am discouraged, Lord, I promise to seek counsel from someone more wise than me. Maybe I can talk to...

_____

_____

_____

_____

_____

_____

May 7

Lou had Alzheimer's disease and his beloved wife, Grace, suffered from a major stroke. He lived in the dementia wing; she in a special care unit of her own.

Lou pretty much kept to himself, but could still walk on his own, so every day a loving caregiver walked Lou over to visit with Grace, whose head hung low, the result of her infirmity. Sometimes he knew her, sometimes not, and vice versa.

One day, as their daughter, Sandie was visiting the two of them, Lou 'came to' for a moment. He looked at his wife, looked at his daughter, and back again to his wife as he demanded, "For Heaven's sake, Gracie, the kids are here. Snap out of it!"

*I realize, Lord, that my expectations are sometimes over the top. And I don't have an excuse! Help **me** to "snap out of it!"*

May 8

Do you feel like you are breaking new ground?
Treading in strange waters?
Going where no man has gone before?

You're not really, you know. It just feels that way sometimes.

Are you fearful? Feeling inadequate? Find someone to talk to – someone who has been a caregiver. Call Hospice. They'll help you.

Then you won't feel so alone.

Lord, I pray today that this dear caregiver will be

able to connect with a friend ASAP!

May 9

We can live as if this life were all we had, as if death were absurd and we had better not talk about it; or we can choose to claim our divine childhood and trust that death is the painful but blessed passage that will bring us face-to-face with our God. *Henri J.M. Nouwen* [6]

The entire family was involved in caring for Grandpa right up to his death.

"Your kids are there with you?"

"Yes, they all came home from school to participate."

"Isn't it discouraging for them? To watch him suffer like that?"

"I don't think so. This is one of the most important things they will ever do. It will teach them more about life than college ever could."

With our children we must:
Dedicate – Educate – Advocate

May 10

She's older than the continental shelf. Her age would make a good bowling score. *Louis DePalma on Taxi*

"Grandma's memory is full." That was the family's way of saying, "Don't expect too much from Grandma anymore." Grandma, at 103 years old, confirmed their notion.

It was a large family wedding. All the kids, grandkids, and great-grandkids were there, as well as one hundred or so close friends. Grandma sat in the seat of honor – the most comfortable chair they could find – flanked on both sides by her daughters.

One of them, Ginger, chatted with her mom about the beautiful bride, the cake, all the trimmings. Grandma nodded along, not saying much until, "By the way, who are you?"

"I'm Ginger, Mom! Ginger!"

"Oh! That's so funny!" Grandma exclaimed, slapping her knee. "Who would name their kid 'Ginger'?"

May 11

There are people who make it happen, people who watch it happen, and people who wonder what happened. *Mike Reagan*

Connie's mom stole socks. That was her 'thing' ever since she got Alzheimer's disease. She would wander into a bedroom, open all the drawers in the chest until she found the socks, stuff them into her apron, and take them to her motor-home for her husband, who spent his days in a wheelchair.

The kids just laughed it off. "Mom's gotten wacky, that's all!" Funny.

But it wasn't funny to Connie. She knew her mom needed help. Soon she would do more dangerous things, and Dad would not be able to take care of her.

So Connie entered into her mother's problem and found both parents a nice apartment near her own home. Rather than 250 miles away, they would be right next-door.

Connie's ten brothers and sisters did not agree with the plan, however. While no specifics were mentioned, they just did not want for Connie to have the say-so. So they grumbled. When questioned, however, no one had a better idea.

God was in it. Her parents were moved nearby, and less than a month later, Connie's dad had a stroke and died. Had

Connie not 'interfered,' Mom would be alone today.

Lord, thank you for the Connies of this world; the caregivers who fight for what is right and good.

May 12

The counselor from Hospice said, "Carrie, you are giving your dad a huge gift by taking care of him as he suffers from Alzheimer's disease." Carrie had never thought of it that way. A gift! She was glad she sought help. Those encouraging words made her day!

Lord, please bless those who encourage me. Thank You for...

_____

_____

_____

_____

_____

_____

May 13

Anybody can grab a tiger by the tail. You only survive by knowing what to do next. *Unknown*

There is no job so simple that it cannot be done wrong.

Lord, help me to discern which jobs I am capable of as a caregiver. Let me know when to seek help.

May 14

Shari's Restaurant after church is usually quite crowded: People filling the waiting room, waitresses hustling about trying to please everyone at once, plenty of impatience to go around.

Linda and her grandmother were sitting at a table for four – just the two of them. She didn't realize when they sat down that the place would fill up so fast. Feeling self-conscious, Linda was trying to hurry the older lady along.

"Have you figured out what you would like to eat, Grandma?"

"No, dear. Not just yet," came the reply.

A few minutes later, "So, Grandma, what looks good?"

No answer.

"Grandma, are you ready to order?" Now tapping her fingers on the tabletop.

"Actually, dear, I'm having a hard time reading the menu today. You see, my eyes aren't my best feature. Walking is my best feature."

May 15

Empty Suit

"Mr. Casey, Janet's father has been taken into the hospital. They don't think he's going to make it through the night. Since you are an elder, I thought maybe you could help."

"Yes, I visited with him earlier this morning. I talked with him about salvation matters, the tenets of the faith."

"Have you talked with the family?"

"Why would I do that?"

"I was thinking that maybe you could provide some comfort for them, too."

"Comfort? Exactly what would that look like?"

~~~

If you see a church leader who is arrogant and pompous, he did not get that at God's store. *Steve Brown*

May 16

Remember! David could not fight the battle in Saul's armor.

Our fellow caregivers can provide us with help and encouragement – good things! God furnishes the rest:

> *"Be prepared. You're up against far more than you can handle on your own. Take all the help you can get, every weapon God has issued, so that when it's all over but the shouting you'll still be on your feet. Truth, righteousness, peace, faith, and salvation are more than words. Learn how to apply them. You'll need them throughout your life. God's Word is an indispensable weapon." Ephesians 6:13-17*

May 17

"Leave me alone. I'm having my own little pity party today."

"Today was such a good day!"

"I've never been so tired, Lord."

"I don't think I've been this angry – ever!"

Oh, Caregiver. Do you feel like you are on an emotional roller coaster? Don't worry; it's like that for all of us.

Just take it a day at a time. If you are down, you'll feel

better soon.

There is no material as resilient as the human spirit.

May 18

"... We continue to shout our praise even when we're hemmed in with troubles, because we know how troubles can develop passionate patience in us, and how that patience in turn forges the tempered steel of virtue, keeping us alert for whatever God will do next. In alert expectancy such as this, we're never left feeling shortchanged... Quite the contrary – we can't round up enough containers to hold everything God generously pours into our lives through the Holy Spirit!" Romans 5:3-4

Dear God, I need patience! I'm thinking specifically about...

_____

_____

_____

_____

_____

_____

May 19

If it's new – it's not true.
If it's true – it's not new.

Hey, Caregiver! Someone has walked in your shoes before.

Networking is a good thing!

May 20

I find that doing the will of God leaves me no time for disputing about His plans. *George MacDonald*

Who would have guessed? When Jerry and Sue decided to take Mom in, they supposed it would be **for a year or two**. They set up a nice room for her, gave her a 'living' area and bathroom of her own, and let her know that they were happy to expand their daily lives to include her.

She was a sweet lady, and had no designs on dominating their time. She was indeed grateful for their love and commitment to her.

After five years or so, her Alzheimer's graduated to the level where she no longer knew who they were. She forgot how to walk, how to feed herself, and how to use the bathroom. She became bed bound.

Four years later, Mom died.

Thank You for the example of Jerry and Sue. Help me, oh Lord, not to limit my service schedule for my own comfort, but to expand my service to include every moment and detail that Your will desires. My time is Your time, God.

May 21

Theology is the study of God and can be overwhelming – because God *is* overwhelming! *Sylvia Jacobson*

Lord, remind me that it is not my job to explain doctrine to this needy one. (I'll leave that to the *professors.) My job is to **show** doctrine – the doctrine of love.*

May 22

Young Peggy's days were full of sorrow; for her mother, Lamantha, was dying from pancreatic cancer. Living out her last days in the nursing home, Lamantha did not complain. She had a family who loved her dearly. In fact, Peggy and her aunt, Helen, were at Lamantha's side around the clock. She was never alone.

When her pastor would visit, he would ask, "How are you doing today?" She would answer her usual, "Fine. Just fine."

"You've always been just fine, haven't you, hon?"

They understood each other, Lamantha and her pastor. For they both knew that Jesus was their Savior, and that the pain and suffering in this life are fleeting compared to eternity with an awesome God.

But Peggy did not understand. She did not understand the assurances that her mother held on to.

As she sat by the bedside, her mother would ask, "Will you read to me, Peggy? How about in the book of Matthew?"

Peggy complied. Day after day, Peggy read to her mom from the Bible until she knew many of the stories by heart.

And then Lamantha died. And then Peggy put down the Bible.

But she did not forget. In later years, in a time of deep need, the stories about Christ's love haunted Peggy until she, too, turned to Him as Savior.

To her dying day, Lamantha witnessed to her daughter. And her faithfulness had eternal consequences!

Can you hear the angels singing? Can you hear a mother's cries of joy?

May 23

I knew I had become my mother today. I didn't have any pockets, so I stuffed my Kleenex up my sleeve. *Audrey Turco*

O God, help me in my youthful arrogance. Remind me in the ways that I will remember, Lord, that I too will some day be old. And..... I might even need a caregiver! Amen.

May 24

We're good friends. So we don't have to play games. We just throw stuff at each other and if it sticks – fine. If it doesn't, we just pick it up and throw it again. *Dottie Bell*

I am so grateful. I can count on this friend as a true blessing in my life...

_____

_____

_____

_____

_____

_____

May 25

Ethel loved to tell stories. She was a witty old lady who enjoyed having an audience. One story in particular she loved to tell, a warm and funny tale about her past.

She decided to relay that great memory to her part-time caregiver. "Have I told you about the time we....?" and off she went.

Midway through the punch line, Ethel paused, then smiled, and with a brush of her hand, said, "Oh, I don't remember the rest. You finish the story."

May 26

"I used to cry a lot. Sometimes I would go swimming so nobody could see the tears." How nice of Laura to tell me that! She made me feel like I was normal.

Sometimes you just need a good friend to share with, don't you? All of your emotions – especially the negative ones – can build up until you feel like you're going to explode.

Then the Lord sends someone along who has been through just what you are going through. And they let you know that you are ok, even if you don't feel ok.

Taking care of a helpless person requires all you have to give, and sometimes more. It's when you get really tired, and angry, and bitter about what you are experiencing that you *must* find someone to talk to, someone who thinks that what you are doing is worthwhile.

So do something for yourself, Caregiver. Find someone who's been there.

AND LET IT ALL HANG OUT!

May 27

Lord, as individual caregivers, our boats are so very small and that ocean is so big! Teach us how to 'buoy up' to each other. Amen.

May 28

*"Do you want to be counted wise, to build a repu-
tation for wisdom? Here's what you do: Live well,
live wisely, live humbly. It's the way you live, not
the way you talk, that counts." James 3:13*

*Lord, thank You for giving me this job at this time
in my life. I needed to humble down, Father. You
knew that.*

May 29

Low Profile – High Impact.

That's you, Caregiver!

Of course, you know about the Low Profile part. You
haven't been in the movies or on the TV news lately. You
have been behind the scenes doing all the 'grunt' work that
is necessary to keep this infirmed one's life going. You are
bathing, dressing, spoon-feeding, medicating, tending to
bathroom duties, reading-to, talking-to, giving nurture to
one who is helpless to perform.

High Impact? Consider the *eternal* results that will flow
from the love you are pouring out. How many lives are you
touching?

Whew! What an important job! You are so appreciated!

May 30

To be growing older is, in some ways, to be still growing. Age is sage.

I have a concern. I'd like to talk about it with...

_____

_____

_____

_____

_____

_____

May 31
Memorial Day

"I can barely cope," said Cheryl. "My mom cannot live alone anymore. She can't cook, she can't drive herself to the store, she can't even take a shower and get dressed without help."

When asked if she is a reluctant caregiver, she says, "No. I want to take care of my mom for the rest of her life. I want to tend to her needs.

"It's just hard to face the fact that I don't have my 'mom' anymore. She doesn't know who I am most of the time. She doesn't make conversation. Ya know? She's here – but she's not. I can talk to her all day long about what is going on with me, and it doesn't matter. She has no suggestions. She doesn't even know what I'm talking about!

"The problem is – I've lost my blanky."

~~~

Oh, Caregiver, is that a tattered, satin edging I see on you? Do you know someone like Cheryl who can hold on to you for a while?

SIX

DUST BUNNIES

Doesn't force itself on others,
Isn't always "me first,"

June 1

My house is so dirty – the flies left. The sink is full of dishes and there are dust bunnies in the corner. But you know what? It doesn't matter. Because this one needs me right now.

My desires seem petty compared to the urgency of this situation. Broken body/broken mind. I cannot imagine the suffering this child of God is bearing daily.

Being a caregiver is a calling that does not come cheaply. It takes everything I have in me! But it is so worth it!

My inconveniences are minor, considering...

June 2

Perhaps it is detachment, a gentle "letting-go," that allows the elderly to break through the illusions of immortality and smile at all the urgencies and emergencies of their past life. When everything is put in its proper place, there is time to greet the true reasons for living. *Henri J.M. Nouwen* [7]

What, Oh Lord, do you have to teach me about life through this infirmed one?

June 3

The old man loved to spend time with his kitten. "Oh, little Callie. So soft. See? She likes to sleep here on my lap."

Sometimes he would forget to let her out of the laundry room in the morning. Or he would forget himself and chase Callie with a broom. Callie learned when to cuddle and when to run!

He would sometimes toss a cigarette package for her,

and she would bat it around the living room. Callie was a perfect companion.

You know why? Because she was warm, forgiving, and easy to please.

There's a lesson there.

June 4

"Mrs. Walker?"

"Yes?"

"This is Roy Jenkins at the assisted living home. I'm wondering if you would be so kind as to stop by and talk with me sometime this week."

"Well, certainly, Mr. Jenkins. Is there a problem?"

"Well, Ma'am, I'm afraid you are going to have to find another living situation for your father. He's just wandering a bit too much for the type of security we can provide here at Harbor Glen Home."

"What did he do now?"

"Well, as you know, he has been found out on the far limits of our facility several times now, but this morning he and another fellow made their way off the property altogether. They were found standing in a crosswalk way down there in front of the Fred Meyer store. They stopped right in the middle of the street, blocking traffic!"

"How did you find them?"

"Well, Ma'am, they had on their orange safety vests with our name embroidered on the front, and some kind soul gave us a call. I'm afraid we just can't risk it anymore."

Isn't that how it goes, Caregiver? Just when you think things are all set, everything changes. You find yourself starting all over again. Take heart. Even when everything around you changes, God remains the same. He is there for you.

June 5

"Gotta get it goin'." That's what Dad would say when he felt antsy. In the earlier days, he would get in his car and drive downtown – to the bank – to the grocery store – out and about.

As the years went by, and he could no longer drive, he would 'venture' from his house to mine just across the driveway.

He had become quite frail, and would "Ooch!" and "Ouch!" the whole time he was walking. His travels had become less than happy for him.

I questioned the validity of his complaints. "Now, Dad, that doesn't hurt." I felt that I was on solid ground, as it were, because I personally cared for his feet, and they were in pretty good shape.

Then, I had occasion to borrow his shoes – for a quick run out to the car. Oh my! Did it hurt to walk across the gravel driveway! Those shoes were merely thin-soled slippers.

And I had brushed Dad off!

Oh, Beloved Caregiver, take heed. Be a listener!

June 6

Perfection is neither more nor less than the soul's faithful co-operation with God.

Lord, there is an area in my life that I need help with...

_____

_____

_____

_____

_____

_____

June 7

Katie had no energy left for her last pick-up of the day. It had been a 60-hour week. But a little gal needed a ride home from Adult Day Care.

After she wearily loaded Carla into the van, the little lady began to chat incessantly. "See the Kleenex cover I'm making?" "You know, Katie, you are a really nice person." "You know what? I am ninety years old." "I have two sons who are pretty good to me." On and on.

Katie was too tired to carry on much of a conversation.

Then Carla surprised her. "Hey, Katie, you know how sin overtakes you? Well, I got the victory and I'm singing praises!"

She started humming a familiar old hymn and was soon singing the words. Katie began harmonizing. What had begun as a humdrum day was ending in joy! The two sang all the way home.

Re-energized, Katie's cup was running over. "Some days are just worth getting up for! When you remember Who to sing about, that is."

June 8

The truly faithful soul accepts all things as a manifestation of God's grace, ignores itself and thinks only of what God is doing.

June 9

Laura was on the verge of panic. While trying to get Steve into the shower, he slipped and fell. His lip was torn and the bruising on his shoulder would surely follow. He had ɔwn hard!

Rushing into the emergency room, Laura was sure he would need stitches.

The doctor in attendance, however, did not seem concerned with Steve. In fact, he talked about Steve as though he wasn't in the room.

"What exactly is Steve's disease called?"

"What makes you think you can take care of him? Shouldn't you be getting more help?"

"Why haven't you been trying to get more money for his care? How about a grant?"

Laura was intimidated and angry. Steve was humiliated.

At the end of the day, Steve got very little doctoring. In fact, the MD barely looked in Steve's direction. No stitches were given. No medication. Just questions and accusations.

Oh, Caregiver! Sometimes it seems that the professionals need more help than the patients, doesn't it? It is OK to be bold when you need help. Speak up to the doctor. Speak up to the social worker. After all, you are not vying for attention for yourself. **This one you care for deserves the very best!**

Like Mama used to say, "Get your ickumpucky up!"

June 10

You are seeking for secret ways of belonging to God, but there is only one: making use of whatever He offers you.
Unknown

Lord, there are machines and gadgets and thingymabobs for almost every job I have in my care-giving day. But what You offer is the reason to even use them. I am here for the long haul, God, because I believe You have offered me this oppor-

*tunity to care for another. I trust that You will use
this season to make me more like Jesus.*

June 11

The worst sorrows in life are not in its losses and mis-
fortunes, but in its fears. *A.C. Benson*

*"Don't fret or worry. Instead of worrying, pray. Let
petitions and praises shape your worries into
prayers, letting God know your concerns. Before
you know it, a sense of God's wholeness, everything coming together for good, will come and settle you down. It's wonderful what happens when
Christ displaces worry at the center of your life."
Philippians 4:6-7*

June 12

The God you can't see is bigger than the giant you can
see. *Dave Rasmussen*
Oh, boy, Lord, do I see a giant!

June 13

I am lost.
I have gone out to find myself.
If I return before I get back,
Please ask me to wait. *Auntie Shirley Allen*

June 14
Flag Day

You only love someone as much as you're willing to be inconvenienced. *Elizabeth Elliott*

*Lord, I consider it such a privilege to serve this one who received his injury while defending **my** freedom. His life in the military has been a true testimony of loving others. I pray that mine will be the same.*

June 15

"Grandpa, what are you doing?" He always stopped at the funniest places. "Let's keep going!"

Oh, boy. Probably another good fishing hole. We must have stopped at fifteen of those already.

But, no, this time he was looking up at the mountainside.

"Do you see that, kids? Do you see that rooster?"

Had Grandpa gone bonkers?

"Look at the snow still left in that ravine. It looks just like a magnificent rooster."

You know, he was right! You had to be looking for it, but there it was: A surprise painting from God!

Grandpa sure knew what was important, didn't he?

June 16

Joanie had been spending her life ignoring her own needs for a year now. She was totally out of the mode of satisfying *her* wants! Taking care of her mom had completely taken over. Being a caregiver was a full-time job.

So today she decided to stop at Starbuck's. She'd been living without lattes for too long. Time to get back to normal.

She pulled into the parking lot. "Mom," she said gently, "I'm going to run into this store for a minute, OK? You stay right here."

Five minutes later, walking back to the car, happily sipping on her Grande Mocha, Joanie realized something was different. Mom was sitting in the back seat now. With a closer look, Joanie could see that Mom's clothes were on inside out. Oops!

June 17

You can tell how big a person is by what it takes to discourage him. *Selected*

He was living his dream life. He had a beautiful wife. Cute kids. And he had just purchased a business in partnership with his friend. All was well.

Until the partners decided to remodel, that is. For some reason, the entire contractor's bill ended up in one name. His partner refused to pay his half, left town, and the business failed.

The law in his state did not allow the separation of personal and business debt. He was forced into bankruptcy. He lost his house, his car, and all of his family's belongings with the exception of $100 to buy a car, a set of dishes and the children's toys.

e important part of this story, however, is what hap-pened next.

He and his wife found new jobs and together they paid back every debt – business and personal. They denied them-selves anything new – no clothes, cars, furniture, nothing! – 'til every penny was paid off!

Lord, what courage my dad had! Please bless him for his honesty as he enters his twilight years. Guide me in my care of him. Remind me to honor him daily. Amen.

June 18

Years may wrinkle the skin, but to give up interest wrin-kles the soul. *Douglas MacArthur*

Lord, I want to make a connection with this suffering one. I fear that we are losing her to depression. Please! Give me some ideas...

June 19

Don't find yourself in the lesser. Lose yourself in the Greater.

June 20

Wow! The month is almost over, and I'm not getting anything done around the house. Taking care of Mom uses up the entire day. It's like having a little kid again!

I guess I should look on the bright side, though. With Mom, I get to walk as slow as I want at the store, and she doesn't ask for candy or take things off the shelves (most of the time).

June 21
First Day of Summer

Created for Commitment

For the eternal substance of a thing never lies in the thing itself, but in the quality of our reaction toward it. If in hard times we are kept from resentment held in silence, and filled with inward sweetness, that is what matters. The event that distressed us will pass from memory as a wind that passes and is gone, but what we were while the wind was blowing has eternal consequences. *A. Wetherell Johnson (founder of Bible Study Fellowship)* [8]

June 22

Dottie's care-giving job consisted of driving the infirmed to where they needed to go – keeping them safe and confident along the way. She packed up one dear little lady's walker and helped her into the transport van. It was her first trip to the valley from this particular adult day care center, and Dottie was not quite sure of how to get there from here. She could rely on her maps if she had to, but the traffic was a bear today, and she hated to look away from the road, so she thought she would ask, "So, dear, you live in the Sumner Valley, right?"

The little lady became concerned, and said she could not possibly help with directions. She wasn't sure where she lived. Her distress became evident.

Dottie consoled her, "I get mixed up too. Lots of times! But you know what I do? I ask God to help me – and sure enough, He does!" Dottie prayed aloud for help. The little lady relaxed.

They successfully made their way to the valley. And after a few "This looks a little familiars," and "Maybe we should turn rights," they were at the lady's doorstep.

"You know what, Dottie? I believe you are right. God does watch over us! I had forgotten about that."

Oh, Caregiver, in the midst of a crowded day, when you don't know which end is up, remember Dottie and the little lady. A simple prayer can do wonders!

June 23

Herb and Stanley were roommates at the nursing home. They spent all their time together – two peas in a pod.

Overheard by their caregiver: "Say, Stanley, why don't you come over and spend the night with me tonight, and then maybe I can come to your place tomorrow?"

June 24

Work like you don't need the money.
Dance like no one is watching.
Love like you've never loved before.

It would be such a blessing if I could just...

_____

_____

_____

_____

_____

June 25

The kids had their friends over after school. For the first time, their teenage buddies met Grandma. She had wandered through the family room a couple of times, and then stopped to ask, "Has anybody seen my laundry?"

"It's probably in the laundry room, Grammy," came the answer. They were used to Grandma's questions – they had been taking care of her for several years now. They recognized the 'stuff' of dementia – the losing things, not remembering names, wandering aimlessly – and were not surprised by them anymore.

But today was different. Today Grandma did something new. As she came back through the room they could see she had indeed found her clothes. She had taken them off and was carrying them!

Ah, Father! As we giggle at the symptoms, help us to take the patient seriously. We want to treat her with dignity, even when she does not remember what dignity means.

June 26

There's no great loss without some gain. *Laura Ingalls Wilder*

June 27

It had been some time since Sally had seen Yola. She noticed that while she could still get around pretty well, Yola barely spoke. She did seem to be enjoying the picnic, though.

Yola's daughter wanted to go for a walk with some other gals, so Sally volunteered to keep her eye on the dear old lady. Sally encouraged the gals to have a nice time on their walk, and "...don't give Yola another thought."

The bar-b-que was cooking away, the salads were all spread out, and Sally decided it would be nice to make up a little lunch for Yola.

With hot dog and potato salad in hand, she sat beside Yola to spoon-feed her.

She did so well! Sally was encouraged and asked her if she wanted seconds. Yola smiled blankly, so Sally brought back another large helping of potato salad.

Half-way through the second helping, Yola looked at up at Sally and asked, "Why are you doing this to me?"

(It seems Yola's daughter had already given her a **huge** lunch!)

June 28

They say that "Time assuages" –
Time never did assuage –
An actual suffering strengthens

As Sinews do, with age –

Time is a Test of Trouble
But not a Remedy –
If such it prove, it prove too
There was no Malady – *Emily Dickinson* [9]

Time *doesn't* heal all wounds, as they say. Some wounds – real wounds – don't go away. They cut deeper into our hearts until we must settle up, one way or another. What really happens over time is that we either grow or we diminish with each cut.

As I look at these old ones – and listen to their stories – I see bitterness in some and utter joy in others. And it all depends on how they have handled their wounds.

Be sure of this! Each one has been wounded. You don't get to be seventy-eighty-ninety without being hurt.

This gets to the very core of what they have believed about life, and about God. If they have received Christ's forgiveness, their response to life will be magnificently different than the response of those who do not know Him.

So I must answer some questions for myself: Will I forgive as I have been forgiven? What will I become?

"Make a clean break with all cutting, backbiting, profane talk. Be gentle with one another, sensitive. Forgive one another as quickly and thoroughly as God in Christ forgave you." Ephesians 4:31-32

Amen.

June 29

I don't believe in frettin' or grievin'.

Why mess around with strife?
I never was cut out to step and strut out.
Give me the simple life.

Some find it pleasant dining on pheasant.
Those things roll off my knife.
Just give me tomatoes or mashed potatoes.
Give me the simple life.

One cottage small is all I'm after,
Not one that's spacious and wide.
A house that's filled with joy and laughter,
And the ones you love inside.

Some like the high road – I'll take the low road,
Free from all care and strife.
It sounds corny and seedy, but yes, indeedy,
Give me the simple life. *H. Ruby, R. Bloom* [10]

Oh, Caregivers! Those old-timers had a handle on this, didn't they? Joy. Laughter. Love.

Imagine how much better we will care for others after we have simplified!

June 30

I am not a victim.
Lord, help me. I need a better attitude about...

_____

_____

_____

_____

_____

SEVEN

THE FAM

Doesn't fly off the handle,
Doesn't keep score of the sins of others,
Doesn't revel when others grovel,

July 1

Some you get along with. Some you don't. Some make you laugh while others make you cry.

Some are dependable. Some more sketchy. True blue. Ne'er do well. Sensitive. Crass.

They make you want to scream sometimes, don't they? I mean, who should you be able to depend on if not the members of the family?

Whether they are your own family – the patient's family – the church family – maybe all of the above, it will drive you crazy if you try to keep track of who is doing the right thing at the right time.

There is a lesson to be learned from the family. A message God has for you: Accept them for who they are. Understand where they are coming from.

Like He does.

July 2

"Hello?"

"Oh, hi, Son!"

"What am I doing? I'm at work, taking care of Margie."

"Dinner? Well, we could have spaghetti. If you would just buzz down to the store to pick up some hamburger and sauce, and, of course, noodles, then we could fix it right up for tonight."

"Oh! And then, will you please put a load in the washer? We really need to get some laundry done."

"Oh yeah! We do need to wash the dog. He really stinks. And we should clean out his house, too, don't you think?"

"What's that? Oh! You're so right, son. Maybe Dad and I should have just named you 'We'!"

July 3

Grace extends value to others beyond our own circle.

July 4
Independence Day

The impulse to pursue God originates with God, but the outworking of that impulse is our "following hard after" Him. *A.W. Tozer*

Oh, Lord, You have made Yourself known to me, and I am trying so hard to follow after You.

Help me to be like you, Jesus. Help me to stay on my feet in this care-giving job. Give me the compassion I need to put this other one first. And teach me forgiveness when no one comes to help.

July 5

When she was harried...
"I've been early of late. I used to be behind before – but now I'm first at last."
About ill-fitted clothes...
"Why don't you have a party and invite your pants down?"
About buying shoes...
"I usually wear a size 7, but an 8 felt so good, I bought a 9."
After she went blind...
"I don't recognize the voice, but the breath is familiar!"
Grandma was a funny lady. Even when she couldn't

remember who we were, she remembered her old sayings that made us laugh.

Look deeply, Caregiver. There are still some original parts there. Treasure the good stuff.

July 6

To be proud of one's virtue
Is its own antidote. *Benjamin Franklin*

Sometimes I puff myself up by putting others down. Lord, I have this confession...

_____

_____

_____

_____

_____

_____

July 7

"...I want you to get out there and walk – better yet, run! – on the road God called you to travel. I don't want any of you sitting around on your hands. I don't want anyone strolling off, down some path that goes nowhere. And mark that you do this with humility and discipline – not in fits and starts, but steadily, pouring yourselves out for each other in acts of love, alert at noticing differences and quick at mending fences." Ephesians 4:1b-3

July 8

The kindness planned for tomorrow doesn't count today.

Oh, Lord. Help me. I keep promising myself that I'll do better next time. But when next time comes, I fail.

When that moment arises, Lord, and I want to put it off just one more time, impress me through the convicting work of the Holy Spirit, God. Don't let me get away with it again. Amen.

July 9

"Stay calm; mind your own business; do your own job. You've heard all this from us before, but a reminder never hurts." 1 Thessalonians 4:11

Good morning, Lord.

I had a tough time last night when I realized that even when I am having a problem, my church family doesn't show up to help. I know I shouldn't keep score, but I woke up today angry and hurt. I hate what this is doing to me. Father, I need to forgive them all.

(I just forgot for a moment that my real Teammate is You!)

July 10

One can live magnificently in this world if one knows

how to work and how to love. *Leo Tolstoy*

Work and love go together, don't they, Lord?

July 11

"Hey, Dan! It's John. I've got a problem, buddy."

"Hey John! What's up?"

"Well, you know I've been taking care of my Dad. And things aren't looking so good. The doctor doesn't think he'll make it through the week."

"Now? I mean, we've already bought the tickets! We can't get a refund now!"

"Dan, my dad is dying."

"People die every day, John. This is the biggest trip of my life!"

"I'm sorry, Dan. You'll have to find someone else."

"WOW! I never imagined you would do this to me. I need you more than your Dad needs you right now."

God, don't let me be a 'Dan.' Teach me to respect others.

~~~

Whoever disenchants
A single Human soul
By failure of irreverence
Is guilty of the whole... *Emily Dickinson* [11]

July 12

The doubter says, "How can this be?"
The believer says, "How *will* this be?"

Oh, God! What a blessing to know you! You know the situation. Please touch the heart of...

_____

_____

_____

_____

_____

_____

July 13

" *Run away from infantile indulgence. Run after mature righteousness – faith, love, peace – joining those who are in honest and serious prayer before God. Refuse to get involved in inane discussions; they always end up in fights. God's servant must not be argumentative, but a gentle listener and a teacher who keeps cool, working firmly but patiently with those who refuse to obey. You never know how or when God might sober them up with a change of heart and a turning to the truth, enabling them to escape the Devil's trap, where they are caught and held captive, forced to run his errands.*" 2 Timothy 2:22-26

July 14

In our country we provide for our elderly. I'm not talking about the government. I am referring to people like you, Caregiver! You are among a special group of individuals who doles out bucket loads of love to those who cannot do it alone anymore. You may be full-time, part-time, a member of the family, the church, or a volunteer organization. You may be a professional. One thing is for sure: You are indispensable!

The salient preservative of our society is the willingness of people to sacrifice for others. It's our Judeo-Christian perspective that keeps it all together.

> *"But you, O God, are both tender and kind, not easily angered, immense in love, and you never, never quit." Psalms 86:15*

July 15

> It would be hard to call what we've been through 'fun,' but I'm sure glad we went through it together. *M-A-S-H*

July 16

He walked into the waiting room at the eye clinic and sat down, heaving a great sigh. His body reflected tension: rigid posture, intense, sad gaze.

The fellow sitting next to him recognized him. "Say, aren't you Mr. Anderson? Don't you live on 3rd Street?"

"Why, yes I am!"

"You are Jim's father, right?"

"Yes."

"I used to go to school with him. How is Jim doing these days?"

"Well, I can't exactly say. I haven't seen Jim in a while."

Just then, the other fellow was called in to see the doctor. Mr. Anderson looked over at me, "I don't see any of my kids anymore. Ever since their mom was diagnosed with Alzheimer's disease, they've dropped off the face of the earth."

"I'm so sorry. My dad just died from dementia," I said, nodding. "It's rough, huh?"

"It sure is; especially because I'm taking care of her by myself. I have a nurse who comes in for two hours each week to give me a break, but that's about it." He was bitter.

"Two hours? You need more time off than that!"

"Yes, but my wife gets so angry when I leave. She swears at me and hits at me, and I feel guilty upsetting her. So... I just stay home."

"Mr. Anderson, here is my phone number. My husband and I would be happy to give you some respite time."

He was then called in to the doctor – and that was the last time I saw him. He never called us. His guilt would not allow him to.

~~~

Oh, Caregiver, are you overtired and overwhelmed? Are you alone because of family members who are no-shows? Understand that taking a break is not a betrayal of your loved one.

Talk to God. Take consolation from Him. He will never leave you or forsake you! In fact, He'll probably send in the troops! Take the help when it's offered.

July 17

One of the hardest things about dying is having to deal with people who don't know how to behave in the presence of death, who lose all sense of what it means to be a human being with limits, who under the provocations of death forget how to live and love, who flee from the mystery of death and in so doing desert the dying person. *Eugene* Peterson[12]

Lord, keep me strong in the face of my loved one's imminent death. Even if the rest of the family avoids the deathbed, O God keep me here. Without You, I am afraid that I, too, will shrink away.

July 18

Teach the Gospel always.
Use words, if necessary.

Thank you, God, for the promise of the Good News. Let this one see Jesus in me so that she, too, might have hope...

_____

_____

_____

_____

_____

_____

July 19

Beautiful faces are they that wear
The light of a pleasant spirit there;
Beautiful hands are they that do
Deeds that are noble, good and true;
Beautiful feet are they that go
Swiftly to lighten another's woe.
McGuffey's Second Reader [13]

Help me to love, Lord, that I may lighten another's woe today!

July 20

Pull gently on a weak rope. *Borrowers Afield*

Dori could not for the life of her understand why her cousin Melissa wasn't coming around. Hadn't Melissa depended on *her* during important times? Hadn't they always been close?

Now that Grandma was dying, Dori needed all the help she could get. Besides the sadness associated with death, Dori had the physical struggles as well: medicating, spoon-feeding, and changing diapers. WHERE WAS MELISSA????

It was true that Dori had been Gram's caregiver all these years, but that did not make this season easier! Now she was facing death issues!

There was one day when Melissa came over for about ten minutes. She said she was going home to change her clothes and would come back to pitch in, but she didn't come back. What on earth was going on?

Oh, Caregiver, don't be too discouraged when someone in the family doesn't show up. Some people really cannot face death. Rather than being angry, pray for her. She may be at the end of her rope.

July 21

Families are like banks. If you take out more than you put in, they go broke.

July 22

He had been awarded the Purple Heart for his heroic service in Vietnam. He had taken a piece of shrapnel in the spine. As a result, he could no longer walk.

As he grew older, his legs began to have spasms; sometimes they would jerk and twitch incessantly.

"Grandpa, can you get out of your wheelchair?"

"No, son, I can't walk anymore. My injury, you know."

"Well, maybe you can't walk anymore, Grandpa, but boy, you sure can dance!"

Grandchildren: The family encouragers.

July 23

He was the skeptic:

"So, you really think God arranged for that to happen?"

"Exactly what are you thanking God for, anyway? Do you really believe He intervened for you?"

His mom did not have good answers. It's hard to prove, you know.

She began to pray for a double-header: that her son would recognize God in everyday life and that her own dad would do the same. A few weeks before he died, hard-nosed old Grandpa believed, and her son did, indeed, hear the angels singing.

So, will God be upset with you if you give Him too much credit? You know the answer to that one, Caregiver. He answers you every day, doesn't He?

July 24

I'm impatient and I'm cussing now. Lord, take the energy in my anger and put it to some good use!

Maybe I should...

_____

_____

_____

_____

_____

_____

July 25

Mama always said:
"If there's a will – I want to be in it!"
"Be nice to your kids – they'll choose your nursing home!"
"Always remember you are unique – just like everyone else!"
"Once I had a handle on life – but it broke!"

She also used to say:
"Put yourself in their shoes."

July 26

It may be your reality, but it's not the truth. *Selected*

Picture a wall. It is made of wooden framing. It has insulation between the studs and is covered over by sheetrock. It is a load-bearing wall and holds up the front end of your roof system. The wall is there. If it weren't there, the building would collapse.

One might say, "There is no wall. I have considered the possibility of the wall, and have decided (after all, I am an intelligent human being) that the wall does not exist."

That's fine. But when encountering the wall, as in trying to walk *through* the wall, one suddenly and most affirmatively discovers that the wall is there!

That's how it is with God. He holds us up, even when we don't acknowledge Him.

Lord, I ask that this suffering one would discover that You are there today.

July 27

"Mommy," said Sarah, "tell me about Mr. Steve. Why is he in that wheelchair?"

"Well, honey, Steve has a bad disease. It's called Machado-Joseph Disease. It fights against his nervous system. It makes him unable to control his body."

"Is that why his hands and legs move funny sometimes?"

"Yes. He can't stop his limbs from moving that way. Did you notice that he has a seat belt on his wheelchair?"

"Yes."

"That's to help hold him in."

"If I hug Mr. Steve, will I catch his disease?"

"Oh, no, Sarah. Hugging Steve is a good thing! He is not contagious. You see, he was born with the disease. It's in his genes. His mother had the disease, too. It's a very sad way that Steve has to live. And the doctors have no cure."

"But, Mommy! There *is* a cure!"

"Oh, honey, it would be so nice if there was – but there really is no cure."

"Yes there is, Mommy! Heaven! Heaven is the cure!!!"

Thank You, Lord, for this little reminder:

Some day! Some glorious day...

"But there's far more to life for us. We're citizens of high heaven! We're waiting the arrival of the Savior, the Master, Jesus Christ, who will transform our earthy bodies into glorious bodies like his own. He'll make us beautiful and whole with the same powerful skill by which he is putting everything as it should be, under and around Him."
Philippians 3:20-21

July 28

Lord, she doesn't come around to help. This is really her job! Yet, I am doing all the work. And it hurts! I want to chastise her!

Then Your Spirit moves, convincing me that my pain, although great, is not equal to what she is suffering. If she could be here, she would be.

I will not question a broken heart.

July 29

There is no testimony without a test!

"No test or temptation that comes your way is beyond the course of what others have had to face. All you need to remember is that God will never let you down; he'll never let you be pushed past your limit; he'll always be there to help you come through it." 1 Corinthians 10:13

July 30

Everybody has a relationship with Jesus:
To some – Judge.
To some – Savior.

Lord, my family needs you. You know the hearts. You love them. Please touch...

_____

_____

_____

_____

_____

_____

July 31

Dad died. After the funeral, a 'concerned' person from our church family called and told me that he had probably gone to hell.

Stunned, I hung up the phone and cried. "Why did she do that? What did she know? She hadn't even seen him in twenty years!" She had been acquainted with him in the past – his not-so-righteous past – and had come to her own conclusion.

She hadn't witnessed the transition after God took hold of him! And she didn't care to hear about it! Plus! She didn't care how much she hurt me!

I wanted to shout it from the rooftop: "I Have Been Wronged! I Am Hurt!"

And I thought I heard Jesus say, "Me, too."

EIGHT

DAY BY DAY

Takes pleasure in the flowering of truth,
Puts up with anything,
Trusts God always,
Always looks for the best,

August 1

There is nothing humdrum about this job. I'm surprised every day, sometimes by good things - sometimes not so good. But even during the challenging times, I find a little something – a little nugget from the Lord.

When the job is messy? Even disgustingly so? I learn Kindness and Humility.

When the one I am serving is ornery? I learn Patience.

You see? He lets me see a glimmer of the Truth: that being in service for Him, no matter how difficult, carries abundant reward – I become more like Jesus.

August 2

Recent 'conversations':

So, Dad, shall we watch a little TV tonight?
Tonight? Bomight? Endight?

~~~

Take me home now.
Well, Dad, the doctor wants you to stay overnight so he can adjust your medicine.
Hey! I had the baby – let's go!

~~~

Open wide, Dad, it's time for a 'calming down' pill.
It's been locked all the way to Mexico.

~~~

Here kitty, nice kitty. (petting a pillow)

~~~

Your son-in-law will be here soon to pick you up, Mr. Meyers.

Where's he gonna go to get the peanuts?

~~~

David is gonna take you into the bathroom now, Dad.

It doesn't matter; they don't have any cake.

~~~

Having trouble communicating, Beloved? Talk to God. Go ahead! Talk right out loud!

This suffering one won't be hurt by your prayers.

August 3

Pain is God's megaphone. *C.S. Lewis*

Maggie used to go to church sometimes. She did it for the kids. They needed a good upbringing, and she was a good mother. Her interest waned when the kids moved away, and she soon drifted from the Sunday meetings.

She enjoyed a challenging job with good pay. She and her husband took nice vacations and had nice friends.

As time passed, the friends drifted away or died. And it became just the two of them. And soon her life-long partner died. And she was alone.

Then, stroke. Agony. Inability.

She cried out, "Oh, God. If You are up there, please let me know! I can't take this anymore!"

Her caregiver was a good listener. She heard the pain. And she knew that God did, too.

They began to attend church together, and for the first time in her life, Maggie surrendered to her Loving Lord.

(And we wonder why God allows pain!)

August 4

I am doing my best. I really am.

But Lord, I've just about had it! I've been accused of not caring, not being 'Christian,' not paying enough attention to the panic and anxiety, and in general, not having a loving attitude. I am tired of the angst and the anger and bitterness that are aimed at me when I am not the source of the problem.

Oh, God, I can barely cope! I am hurt by the injustice here. I feel like I am becoming a basket case!

I tell myself over and over again... if I'm a basket case, at least I'm YOUR basket case.

Oh! Oh my! It has just occurred to me... Is she......Your.....basket case, too?

Oh, Beloved and Bedraggled Caregiver,

Do you feel unappreciated today? Is someone angry with you for no reason?

Take heart! God is not mad at you!

In fact, He is quite pleased with you. You are right on track. You are doing His work! You are caring for *another* one of His basket cases.

"Anyone who meets a testing challenge head-on and manages to stick it out is mighty fortunate. For such persons loyally in love with God, the reward is life and more life." James 1:12

August 5

The kids took Grandpa to the barbershop. He used to go alone, but couldn't find the way anymore.

He had a good time. The barber could not speak much English, but they did just fine, because Grandpa didn't even notice. He just carried on his end of the conversation.

As he checked his new 'look' in the mirror, he said, "Fine. It's just fine." Reaching into his wallet, he pulled out a twenty-dollar bill for his $8.50 haircut.

"Keep the change," he said, as he pulled on his jacket.

"Oh, no! Too much!" declared the barber.

Not wanting to steal their Grandpa's thunder, the kids signaled that it was ok.

The next time Grandpa needed a haircut, they pulled into the parking space, and noticed through the window that every seat was full inside. They began to pull away, when the barber came running out to greet them.

"You first, sir! You first!"

They might have been suspicious that the barber was greedy, but the kindness in his eyes toward Grandpa said otherwise. He understood. And he wanted to honor this generous old man.

Oh, Lord, teach me to honor my elders.

August 6

Leisure is a beautiful garment, but it will not do for constant wear. *Unknown*

Lord, I confess that I'm not finding joy in my work. Help me to look for the best, especially when...

_____

_____

_____

_____

_____

_____

August 7

Time to grow up. Some days we made love together. Other days we had to work at it. You never see the hard days in a photo album. But those are the ones that get you from one happy snapshot to the next. (*in the movie "Just Married"*)

August 8

OK, God. I agreed to take care of her and I really want to. But I have limits, You know? I never said I would change diapers. I don't think I can.

What if I get started and can't go through with it? What if there is no one around to help? Then what?

YOU SEEM TO FORGET – I'LL BE RIGHT HERE. IN FAITH, JUST PUT YOUR FEET IN, AND I WILL PART THE WATERS FOR YOU. REMEMBER THE

LEVITE PRIESTS?

August 9

Ya know what, Dad? There is no one else in the room but us. I talked to the doctor today, and he's going to give you some medicine to make those other guys go away, ok?

~~~

I know it hurts, but we're going to have a therapist come in and help you exercise your arm and leg so you can walk again, ok?

~~~

Dad, I know you're a modest man, but I'm going to have to change you sometimes, if that's ok. It's hard for me to get you into the bathroom lately, and you've been forgetting to tell me when you have to go. So, we'll just start wearing this special underwear, ok?

~~~

I understand that it's hard for you to sleep now. I'll ask the doctor for some more medicine. I'm glad those other guys in the room are not scaring you anymore, but I sure wish the medicine would make them go away for good. It's so hard to get your attention these days.

~~~

Am I leaving soon for work? No, I quit my job, Dad. Well, so I can spend more time here with you.

Why? Well, because I love you, Dad, and I don't want you to be afraid. I'm here for you. I'm hoping that things will settle down for you, and I can talk to you about Jesus. And maybe you'll understand that He was hurt, too, and that He understands how you feel.

"For the present, I'm staying right here... A huge door of opportunity for good work has opened up here." 1 Corinthians 16:8-9

August 10

Life is a trial – mile-by-mile.
Life is so hard – yard-by-yard.
Life is a cinch – inch-by-inch.

August 11

A preacher used to order ice cream and pound cake for lunch when he visited a certain deli. Why would anyone order dessert for lunch?

Why not?

Caregiver, every now and then, let her indulge. And you join her. Make a party out of it. It will probably add time to both your lives!

August 12

Blessed are they who can laugh at themselves for they shall never cease to be amused. *Unknown*

God, thank You for humor! I can't believe what I did the other day...

_____

_____

_____

_____

_____

_____

August 13

"Adam!"

"Adam! Over here!" His caregiver was shouting.

Adam had climbed out of the exercise pool and into the main pool – walking determinedly through the water, crossing the swim lanes. He was drawn to the laughter of kids his own age.

This autistic boy, who generally paid attention to no one, sought to join in with others!

His caregiver, although distressed that he was interrupting the flow of events at the YMCA, was nonetheless overjoyed with this new knowledge – Adam was hearing everything that went on around him! For the first time, he responded to stimulation!

Oh, Caregiver, this one you tend to may appear to be tuned out. But take heart! She might be hearing you, after all.

August 14

Warning: Exhaustion is Self-pity's little sister.

Hey, Caregiver! Get some respite help. Do something

for YOU today.

August 15

It was Shirley's first time working the night shift. Most of the residents had already dropped off to sleep. She checked from room to room – just to be sure everyone was tucked in.

Little Elsie lay on her bed, eyes wide open. "Dear," she whispered ever so softly, "May I use the restroom?"

"Sure, Elsie," Shirley replied, helping her to sit up in the bed.

"Should I stand up now?"

Shirley gently took Elsie's arm, easing her onto both feet.

"Should I walk now?" They slowly made their way to the bathroom.

Shirley got Elsie situated and said, "Elsie, I'm going to step outside to give you some privacy."

"That will be wonderful, dear," came the reply.

After five minutes or so, Shirley tapped lightly on the door. "Elsie how are things going?"

"Splendidly, dear. Just splendidly. But I do have one question. Should I tinkle now?"

~~~

It's all in the details, isn't it?

August 16

Yesterday, he said, "You're a lovely girl."

Today I made him his favorite – French toast. I put lots

of butter and syrup on it – just the way he likes it. He had a cup of cocoa on the side and he truly enjoyed his first meal of the day.

After breakfast, Rich told him it was bath time – something he hated with a passion. For some reason he was fearful of the water, and it was all Rich could do to get him in the tub.

I made him a bologna sandwich with sweet pickles on it for lunch. Another favorite.

Then Rich had him soak his feet and he clipped his toenails – a somewhat painful experience for Dad.

After a dinner of all his favorite stuff prepared by me, Rich made him exercise his previously broken arm. It was not a good experience.

Before bedtime, the three of us sat on the deck to enjoy the sunset.

Dad looked at Rich and said, "I love you."

He looked at me and said, "You, I'm not so crazy about."

August 17

Denial is a nasty foe. It robs you of living a real life. It snatches the pain off the surface and shoves it deep down inside.

Helen has cancer. In her lungs, her breasts, her brain. When asked about the doctor's prognosis, she answers, "He's not telling me anything."

That couldn't possibly be true, could it?

Day after day she resists.

"Helen, I'd like to come over and stay with you awhile."

"No, I really don't need anyone to stay with me."

"Helen, how about if we come over for an hour or so to pray and sing with you?"

"Oh, no. No, I'm not ready for that."

Helen has no family nearby. We are her church family. Once a people-lover, she is now pushing us away. Why?

She doesn't want us to see her life slipping away. If she doesn't let us see, then she won't have to look, either.

She is denying herself friendship in her moment of greatest need.

So, what do I do now? Do I just back off?

I know that God is watching and that He is intimately involved with Helen.

I will wait to hear His voice.

When You give me the word – I'm goin' in, Lord. I know You don't want her to be alone.

August 18

Look at the bright side – you burn up a lot of calories jumping to conclusions! *Unknown*

Lord, I praise You for helping me to see things more clearly. Like this week, when...

_____

_____

_____

_____

_____

_____

August 19

The baby girl was eight months old when she stopped progressing. She had just begun to get up on her knees to rock back and forth - hopeful signs of crawling soon. But then it stopped. She not only did not crawl, she did not get up on her knees again. Her mother was in denial at first, but when she could no longer fake it she began to seek the advice of doctors.

"Did you drink during your pregnancy?" she was asked. "How about drugs?"

"You know, you lived in a badly polluted area when you were carrying this baby."

Was this her fault? Could she have prevented the daily pain her daughter suffered? Had she somehow caused this seemingly hopeless situation?

Bitter pills to swallow: Guilt and Despair.

Eventually her daughter was diagnosed properly. She has Rett's Syndrome. This was not preventable.

Little Ruthie is now seven years old and helpless. She cannot eat alone, move about alone, use the bathroom or bathe. She requires total care morning, noon and night.

Her mom cries a lot, but has a firm resolve to keep going. And although she sometimes feels isolated, her love for her little girl outweighs all other emotions.

Ruthie can do one thing: She says "Ma" (Mommy) and "Va" (love).

To one caregiver, that means everything in the world.

*Lord, help **me** to appreciate the small things.*

August 20

Uncle Charlie was always a funny guy. Well known in his little town in Montana, folks knew who to look for if they found an extra prime rib roast in their shopping cart when they got up to the checkout stand. "Charlie Mickelson!" they would call out. "Where are you?" And they would laugh.

He had great charm and knew how to make people happy. When he traveled, he sent himself postcards from movie starlets, thanking him for the wonderful time. The guys at the post office loved to read them. They would hang them on the wall in the office. "Oh, that Charlie!"

When Charlie got cancer, the whole community knew that they would be losing a beloved friend, indeed.

As sick as he was, my uncle stayed outside of himself, concerned about the well being of others. Two weeks before he died, he called me to ask if there was anything he could do for me before he went. Crying, I asked him to share with others the reason why he was not afraid to die.

My Uncle Charlie believed in a Loving God, a Redeeming Savior. He knew he was Heaven-bound. And God honored Charlie by giving him the faith to carry on – to his dying day.

August 21

You cannot hear the healing confessions at the bedside – confession of love, confession of failure – if you are not at the bedside.

August 22

Both of our dads are gone now. And both of them wanted to talk – have real communication – before they went into eternity.

You know what they talked about? What struck each of them in their final days?

God's beautiful creation.

One dad talked about the flowers in the garden; the other

– the butterfly on the deck. Imagine that!

They had each been 'big' men in their day. Accomplished. Achieving a certain degree of notoriety in their communities.

But in the end, they were drawn to beauty. God was calling them to it. A foretaste of what was to come when they joined Him.

August 23

As I neared the fish counter, I could hear, "I'm sorry Ma'am. I do apologize. I was just trying to help."

What was going on? Coming around the end of the aisle, it became quite clear. There was Auntie June, cranky as ever, chastising a helpful store clerk.

Why does she do that to people?

Embarrassed, I turned and pushed my cart the other way, pretending that I did not know her.

She's mean to people, and in my pride, I don't want them to think I am connected to her. I hate it that she affects me so much. I think she is actually changing who I am! Bringing out the worst in me!

And then You come along and whisper in my ear, God, and I realize that Auntie doesn't get to have that kind of influence over me. Only You do. And because of that truth, she does not threaten me. So I will stick it out as her caregiver.

"Whatever I have, wherever I am, I can make it through anything in the One who makes me who I am." Philippians 4:13

August 24

If all the year were playing holidays, to sport would be as tedious as to work. *William Shakespeare*

I love my free time. I thank God for my work, too. My favorite part of the job is...

_____

_____

_____

_____

_____

_____

August 25

Sundowners. That's what the professionals call it. It's when an infirmed one with Parkinson's disease or Alzheimer's or other dementia gets real cranky and starts seeing things as night draws near. They can get real mean at that time of day, can't they, Caregiver?

It makes you want to just get out of the way. But, of course, you can't. So you pray...

Dear God, please don't let tonight be a bad one. Allow this suffering one to have some peace of mind, and give me the strength to stick it out if she doesn't.

August 26

No wonder his wife was fooled! Mr. Abbott looked dignified. He held himself well.

Mrs. Abbott was upset that he wasn't eating more. It was

hard to explain to her that he was losing the ability to eat. She refused to go there. She could not accept the fact that he was dying.

She brought him custards and chocolate pudding. She coaxed and accused.

He actually did eat something today. But his caregiver didn't have the heart to tell Mrs. Abbott about it. Earlier, she handed him the newspaper to look at while she cleaned up his room.

When she turned her attention back to him, he was eating the paper.

Lord, help me to keep certain experiences to myself: The things that might hurt others. Amen.

August 27

He was so cranky today. Nothing pleased him, and I was about ready to give up, when I remembered why I'm here.

Because of my Heavenly Father, I can love my earthly father. Unconditionally.

August 28

Our greatest glory is not in never falling, but in rising every time we fall. *Oliver Goldsmith*

August 29

I'm not afraid to die. I just don't want to be there when it happens! *Floyd Collins*

Ain't that the truth? None of us does. But for some reason

folks think it's un-Christian to fear death.

If we are Believers in Jesus Christ, we don't have to fear the other side of death, but the process of dying is the pits! For everybody! And we can't put a cheery face on it and pretend that the pain and suffering of death are somehow mitigated by the fact that we are Christians.

As we care for the infirmed, let's recognize the fear for what it is, and admit to ourselves that when we get there, we'll be scared, too.

August 30

Everyone lives between his ears. You are what you think. *Art Linkletter*

I want to see the good in every day. Today's big 'plus' is...

_____

_____

_____

_____

_____

_____

August 31

Blessed be Your name,
In the land that is plentiful,
Where Your streams of abundance flow,
Blessed be Your name.

Blessed be Your name,
When I'm found in the desert place,
Though I walk through the wilderness,
Blessed be Your name.

Every blessing You pour out
I'll turn back to praise.
When the darkness closes in, Lord,
Still I will say...

Blessed be the name of the Lord.

Blessed be Your name,
When the sun's shining down on me,
When the world's all as it should be,
Blessed be Your name.

Blessed be Your name,
On the road marked with suffering,
Though there's pain in the offering,
Blessed be Your name.

You give and take away.
You give and take away.
My heart will choose to say,
Lord, blessed be Your name! *Matt Redman* [14]

NINE

HISTORY LESSONS

Never looks back,
But keeps going to the end.

September 1

He brought this all on himself, you know.

She never was very nice.

Did you hear what he used to do?

Sometimes she would...

Ahhh, the past. Everybody has one. And usually there are sore spots; painful reminders about what didn't go well. There were urgent problems where inappropriate responses were as destructive as the difficulties they sought to overcome.

Life is a series of battles, after all. Some noble. Some, well...

But what are we supposed to do with the past? Shall we relive it, harboring our anger toward this infirmed one? Was the battle five years ago? Did it last an entire childhood? Have old wounds been re-opened? Did the bad history begin just yesterday with a harsh word or some other symbol of ungratefulness?

Beloved, know this: Nothing gets fixed without love. Not a gushy, sentimental love, but commitment/sticking-to-it love.

See this through to the end. If you do, you will be writing a new chapter in the history of the lives involved – in which the successes outweigh the failures – finally!

September 2

He got so mean in his last days. He said terrible things to us. "You are drugging me!" "This is a plot against me!"

He shook his fist at us and gritted his teeth in anger.

He called us names and shouted, "Get me outta here!"

It was awful. And now that he is gone, the bad memories linger.

How do I get around the bad stuff so that I can cherish the good stuff?

~~~

Visualize sweeping up the pieces of your broken heart, sweeping them into the dustpan, and giving them to Jesus. *Dottie Bell*

September 3

The Bible tells us that Barnabas was an encourager.

An encourager:
1. Gives away what God has given him.
2. Listens.
3. Notices the Lord working and tells. ("I see God at work in your life.")

In the past, did someone encourage you? Is there another caregiver who could use a Barnabas today?

September 4

Worry is a thin stream of fear trickling through the mind. If encouraged, it cuts a channel into which all other thoughts are drained. *Steve Brown*

September 5

Father God, as I ponder my yesterdays, one thing is certain: all the sin, sorrow and shame of my past are gone. You took them off my shoulders, Lord. You paid the price. You bore the burden.

You gave me freedom! Freedom to care for this loved one with unconditional love. Amen! and Amen!

September 6

We can buy insurance – but we can't buy assurance.

Lord, help this one I am caring for to make the connection – that You are the source of real security, and not...

_____

_____

_____

_____

_____

_____

September 7

The twins were quite elderly and suffered from diminished mental capacity. They'd been declared retarded in their first year of life, and were given over to the 'system.'

Their loving new caregiver decided to nurture them in a manner they were not accustomed to. So she brought them to church every Sunday. They sat politely, quietly listening to the music. They drew pictures on their bulletins. They smiled at the folks.

Then, one Sunday, they surprised everyone. Whispering at first, and then building to a full-blown concert level, they sang, "Jesus loves me, this I know. For the Bible tells me so!"

Some loving soul in their past *had* nurtured them! Someone had told them about Jesus! What a blessing to continue work that someone else had begun!

"Now the Sower is arm in arm with the Harvester, triumphant. That's the truth of the saying, 'This one sows, that one harvests.'" John 4:36b-37

September 8

We're free to make choices, but we're not free from the consequences of those choices. *Erma Hughes*

September 9

She carried a large handbag with her whenever she visited her daughter's house. As evening drew near, she would wander through the rooms, taking pictures off the walls, knick-knacks off the bookshelves – stuffing them into her bag. "This is mine," she would say. "This is mine." Collecting things. Trinkets from her past.

Of course, there was no room for them at the nursing home, and besides, she had given them to her daughter years ago. But there was something she was trying to recapture here.

What she could no longer realize, due to her dementia, was that her past was not important. Except, of course for that one day. The day her daughter told her about Jesus. About how He would forgive all her sins if she would just ask. She learned about Eternal Salvation.

"This is mine!" she had said. "This is mine!"

September 10

Trapeze

A flyer must fly, and a catcher must catch, and the flyer must trust, with outstretched arms, that his catcher will be there for him. *Henri J.M. Nouwen* [15]

Know Anybody you trust that much, Caregiver? He's there for you. He really is.

September 11

Traveling

Cruising right along. Montana is wide open. Not too many cars on the road. Dad just dozed off. Mom is reading. Peace.

What is that black thing? Just the tread off a tire. No time to move over. I'll just center up over it.

What .... what was that? *Oh, Lord! What did we hit?*

What's that smell? Mom! Dad! Get out of the car quickly! Walk with me. No! Dad! Don't light that cigarette! Just keep walking. Smell that? The fuel tank has ruptured!

The shoulder is soaked in gas!

This way, Dad. This way. Stay with me!

Let's just walk down this little embankment here, ok? Sure you can. No, you won't fall off the edge. (What edge?) Now, Dad, you stay right here and guard Mom, ok? And remember, no smokes! Better yet, why don't you just hand those to me? I'll walk back up by the road and call 911.

No, you won't get heat stroke. It's only 70 degrees out here. Yes, the State Patrol will be here soon.

~~~

The officer gave us a ride back to safety. And what a ride! We flew down the middle of the freeway in the patrol car at 100 MPH, sirens howling!

Completely forgetting what had happened thirty minutes ago, Dad was *enjoying* himself! "Say," he said to the patrolman, grinning from ear to ear, "that's some engine you got in this thing!"

Oh, Boy.

September 12

The old dreams were good dreams – they didn't work out – but I'm glad I had 'em. *Selected*

Thanks, Lord. My dreams kept me going at times. Especially...

_____

_____

_____

_____

_____

_____

September 13

Old Al visited the Coffee Cafe every morning and evening. As he walked through the door, someone would invariably call out "Hey, Al! Grande Mocha?"

Al would smile, relishing the recognition. He would settle into his favorite chair and read the morning paper, occasionally looking up to search the crowd for familiar faces.

He shared his story with anyone who had time to listen.

Recently retiring from his position as a high school counselor, he had many tales to tell. A gentlemen in every sense of the word, Al never pushed his way into conversation, but patiently waited to be noticed.

He would finish his drink and make his way back home – alone. Later on, he would venture out again.

Lord, help me to notice the 'Als' who I come into contact with each day. And then, O God, when they want to chat about their past, give me the presence of mind to take the time to listen.

September 14

The theology of Christianity is grace and the ethic of Christianity is gratitude. *Steve Brown*

Lord Jesus,

Thank You for this work of care-giving. I know Lord that I do not have to dwell on my past. You have covered it. And the muddy past of this suffering one, also. Because of You, we're both looking ahead now.

September 15

A happy childhood can't be cured. Mine'll hang around my neck like a rainbow.

I was loved. And I intend to love.

September 16

If we fill our hours with regrets of yesterday and with the worries of tomorrow, we have no today in which to be thankful.

> *"I'm not saying that I have this all together, that I have it made. But I am well on my way, reaching out for Christ, who has so wondrously reached out for me. Friends, don't get me wrong. By no means do I count myself as an expert in all of this, but I've got my eye on the goal, where God is beckoning us onward – to Jesus. I'm off and running, and I'm not turning back." Philippians 3:12-14*

September 17

OK. So there were some hard times. Sometimes she yelled at me. Sometimes she drank too much. She forgot my birthday a couple of times, too.

That's the truth of it – she wasn't a perfect mom.

Then there is the Jesus factor. *I* messed up and then fessed up and He forgave me every time. Not because I am a perfect child, but because He is a merciful God.

Remembering the truth of my past with her and my future of mercy with Him, it's really a no-brainer:

Truth and mercy have got to join hands and walk together. I will love and care for my mom until the day she dies.

September 18

Some would say that believing in a loving, proactive God is a crutch for the weak. You know what I say? I don't need a crutch – give me a gurney!

Oh, Jesus. I really need You today! Please help me to...

_____

_____

_____

_____

_____

_____

September 19

I've been around for a lot of days.
I've looked at life in so many ways.
I've seen it all, the lows and the highs.
Been down to the bottom, and reached for the skies.

I've traveled around to all kinds of towns.
I've cried with the sinners, and laughed with the clowns.
I've looked the world over for fortune and fame,
But you won't find a soul who remembers my name.

I've found it takes heartache to know how to live.
A man that's a fool doesn't know how to give.
I've learned when you dance to a selfish tune,
The Fiddler must be paid.

So Life, before you go,
There's one more thing I'd like to know:

When was that moment,
That one special moment,
When I was what I was born to be? *Bob Mickelson* [16]

Oh Lord Jesus, help me to affirm this suffering one today. I want him to know that he was born to be Your child! He needs Your love and forgiveness before he passes into eternity. Amen

September 20

I skate to where the puck is going to be, not where it has been. *Wayne Gretzky*

September 21

An Unmade Bed of a Guy

Lord, I can't believe how incompetent Dad is. He is helpless.

He can't change a light bulb.

He can't button his sweater. Zip up his coat.

He eats with the wrong end of his fork!

Dad, when was the last time you brushed your teeth? Washed your hair?

He's wearing the same sweater every day. Shredded elbows. He spends an hour in the bathroom getting 'cleaned up.' What on earth is he doing in there? When he shaves he misses every-thing on the underside of his chin (sort of a "Seven Dwarves" look).

Dad is literally coming apart.
*The truth of it is: We are both doing as much as we can. He is making his way through the day **in** his own cloud, and I, watching him, am walking it would seem, **under** a cloud.*

How did this happen? When did it start? Is there something I could have done? Is there something he should have done?

And You gently nudge me and say, "It doesn't mat-ter, child. Don't look back. Look at Me. I will give you both a future and a hope."

September 22
First Day of Autumn

Lord, when this suffering one begins to cry, especially about a past which neither of us can do anything about, what can I say?

The past has been sordid. There is guilt. Dreams were dashed. How do I respond? Especially when there is reason for the guilt and emptiness.

"Be gracious in your speech. The goal is to bring out the best in others in a conversation, not put them down, not cut them out." Colossians 4:6

September 23

Sin will always take you farther than you want to go,
Make you pay more than you want to pay,
Make you stay longer than you want to stay. *Dottie Bell*

September 24

It is ridiculous to assume that Satan drowned at your baptism. *Jerome*

My prayer for today and all of my tomorrows is that I won't rest on the good I accomplished *yesterday*. I still need to...

_____

_____

_____

_____

_____

September 25

Forbidden Fruits Create Many Jams.

She was experimenting with drugs. She had sex with many partners. She did exactly what she wanted to do and nobody could stop her from having fun! Authority was out the window. Her moral compass was out of tilt. Nobody cared. It was the Sixties and she was 'hip.'

Then she got pregnant and the doctor warned her, "Your baby may be deformed. Drugs can do some terrible things to a fetus. You may want to find an abortionist. It's illegal, but I can give you some information."

A fetus? It hit her right between the eyes. This was a **baby** they were talking about! I mean – she would experiment with many things, but not her little baby! Had her behavior caused others to think that even human life was not important to her anymore?

She told the doctor, "Thanks, but no thanks. I am carrying this baby to full term!"

As the doctor predicted, her little boy was born with Spina Bifida. His spine was unprotected in one area and badly damaged. He would never walk. Some of his internal organs could not function normally. He was a very sick child.

But his mother got healthy in ways she could not have imagined. This young, rebellious mom became a caregiver overnight. She gave up her partying days to become a servant. Finally, she was making right choices! It paid off. Her little boy drew out of her a love she didn't think she had in her. And she loved him until the day he died.

> *God, help me to make right choices when I'm asked by You to give up my comforts so that another might survive. Teach me to choose life, Lord.*

September 26

Will I ever fail God as I care for others?
Of course I will fail!

I'm not depending on my goodness – but His!

Count yourself lucky, how happy you must be –
you get a fresh start,
your slate's wiped clean.

Count yourself lucky –
God holds nothing against you
and you're holding nothing back from him.

When I kept it all inside,
my bones turned to powder,
my words became daylong groans.
The pressure never let up;
all the juices of my life dried up.

Then I let it all out;
I said, "I'll make a clean breast of my failures to God."

Suddenly the pressure was gone –
my guilt dissolved,
my sin disappeared. Psalms 32:1-5

September 27

The number one factor toward emotional recovery is the knowledge you are not alone.
I'm still here, Mom. I'm not going anywhere.

September 28

They Can't Take That Away From Me.

Daddy's home! Did you talk on the radio today, Daddy? I like hearing you on the radio.

~~~

My friend says Mommy is pretty. And my Daddy is

handsome!

~~~

My Daddy sits and watches the fights on TV with me every Friday night. We eat smoked oysters and crackers. Then he goes out with the band.

~~~

My Daddy plays piano. And saxophone. And bass. And drums. And xylophone. He's so smart!

~~~

Grandma bought me a horse named Sugar! She's real pretty. But she's sassy. Daddy said he would ride her to show her who's the boss. I never saw a horse buck so hard! Poor Daddy! He's not a very good cowboy. But he said everything will be ok. He always says that.

~~~

I get to be in the talent show! Will you teach me how to sing, Daddy?

~~~

Daddy and I ate liver tonight. We like it. Daddy and me are buddies.

~~~

Daddy wrote a song for me. He made a record.
Are we famous?

I like the words to your songs, Daddy. You always write about love.

~~~

You are my Daddy. And I am a happy little girl.

Lord, thank you for my childhood. It made it easier to care for others.

September 29

Looking back, I cannot remember when I've had a more consuming job.

I am in a situation in which another person is required to fully trust in me. Imagine that. And I must prove myself to be true blue. Not in the will-you-be-mine-forever? way, but in the will-you-pick-me-up-feed-me-medicate-me-dress-me-help-me-use-the-toilet-because-I-cannot-do-it-alone way. It's close and tough and private.

There's not much I can say at the end of a day. I'm not winning any wars. Just small battles which will be repeated tomorrow and tomorrow and tomorrow.

The daily doings of this one who is suffering have become my doings. The nourishment, enterprise, and encouragement are mine to supply. It's literally do or die.

Lord, help me be up to this task. I'm feeling over-whelmed right now.

September 30

Not many wise and not many mighty come into the

Kingdom of God. *Unknown*

Oh God, I praise You for who You are. Thank You for keeping me in my place. Especially when...

_____

_____

_____

_____

_____

_____

TEN

MY WAY OR YAHWEH?
The Heart of the Matter

Inspired speech will be over some day; praying in tongues will end; understanding will reach its limit. We know only a portion of the truth, and what we say about God is always incomplete. But when the Complete arrives, our incompletes will be canceled.

When I was an infant at my mother's breast, I gurgled and cooed like any infant. When I grew up, I left those infant ways for good.

October 1

"I'd rather be sailing."
"I'd rather be fishing."
"I'd rather be shopping at Nordstrom's."

You've seen the bumper stickers. You've nodded in agreement; chuckled while mentally filling in "I'd rather be..." with your own favorite pastime.

The reason those slogans are so popular is obvious: Of course you'd rather be playing than working!

But that's wishing for infant's milk, isn't it? And you're all grown up now.

Caregiver, you have been given a job to do. It's not as fun as fishing, but the catch is more important: You just might win this one for the Kingdom of God! It's not as fun as sailing, but it will get you farther: The destination is eternal!

God has put this helpless one in your life, Beloved.

October 2

Every Monday, Wednesday and Friday they showed up at the YMCA – some by transport vans, some by private car. The stroke victims.

They went through the rigors of 'in-pool' leg and arm exercises for an hour, some more adept than others, each one giving it her all.

At the end of the session, they lined up at one corner of the pool. Laughing, chatting (if they were able), each waited her turn in the chair lift. Most of them could not walk!

But they carried on. Maturity had taught them that it's not over 'til it's over.

There wasn't a Quitter in the bunch!

October 3

Yola couldn't do much around the house anymore. She couldn't remember how the vacuum worked. She would forget which dishes were washed and which were still dirty. But her daughter discovered something that Yola could still pull off!

"Mom," said Sue, "let's pick some berries. We're having a big party this weekend, and it would be so nice to have some blackberry pies!"

So, brown bags in hand, they set out to gather their harvest. They must have picked five pounds of berries that afternoon!

"Time to clean them up, Mom."

Sue turned on the tap at the kitchen sink. "I'll carefully take them out of the bags and put them in this strainer, ok? And you can rinse them off and dump them into this bowl. All right?"

"All right!"

They busied themselves for the next hour or so.

They were almost finished when the phone rang. Sue excused herself to answer it, and when she returned, Yola had taken all but a half-pound of the berries and shoved them down the garbage disposal!

The company enjoyed their small portions of berry (and apple) cobbler that evening, and Yola was pleased as punch!

"We did our best, didn't we, Mom?"

"Yes. We did our best."

Don't sweat the small stuff, Caregiver. Like Sue, you are doing a wonderful job! It's just that sometimes the joy has to be in the doing, and not the outcome.

October 4

We gazed upon his ashen face and clenched, gnarled hands with sadness. Dad was leaving us. We whispered to him our "thank yous" and "goodbyes" and thanked God the Father that we would see Dad again.

For, in His mercy and grace, He received Dad as one of His own.

Dad never said the appropriate sinner's prayer – he could not speak.

He did not go forward during an altar call – he did not attend that type of church.

But we could see surrender in his eyes when we talked about Jesus. And that's all he needed to do – surrender.

October 5

Jesus is God's conversation with us in a language we can understand. And He came for "whoever."

Cannot walk? "Whoever." He will pick you up.

Cannot speak? "Whoever." He will touch your mind.

Cannot hear? "Whoever." He will break into your very soul.

He came for this helpless one. He came for the cranky one – the incontinent one – the one who just sits and stares.

Jesus is God's conversation with us in a language we can understand, the language of unconditional love.

October 6

Life's most urgent question is: what are you doing for others? *Martin Luther King*

Beginning right now, I promise to...

_____

_____

_____

_____

_____

_____

October 7

Hazel and Betty were lesbians. Everyone in the neighborhood knew it. They were invited to the neighborhood block parties each year, but otherwise were left alone.

Everyone would see them coming and going: to work, to the store. There would be polite smiles and waves, but no real friendship.

Then one neighbor, Jenni, realized that she hadn't seen Betty in awhile. She decided to drop by to inquire, only to hear the bitter news: Betty was dying of cancer.

"Who is helping you take care of her, Hazel?"

"It has been just me. But she's in the hospital now. She doesn't have long."

Jenni decided to take care of the caregiver. She began to visit with Hazel on a regular basis. She invited her into her home often.

Hazel eventually shared her story, the deep pathos of her tragedy.

Jenni loved her and listened to her and cried with her.

That's what Jesus would have done.

October 8

Maturity is seeing a sunrise or a sunset and knowing Who to thank.

October 9

He lost the power.
Fantastic husband, lover. Age slowed him down.
Great dad. Superhero. The kids were all grown.
On the 'inside' at his workplace. Now retired.
Unapproachable jazz musician. Couldn't put the sax together anymore.
But he was a lucky man. For it was only after he lost *his* power, that he began to understand the power of God in a broken life.

October 10

Born OK the first time. (*bumper sticker*)
(Yeah, right. And then someone taught you how to be selfish when you became a toddler.)

The Birthmarks of a Born-*Again* caregiver are:

1. Righteousness
2. Love
3. Sacrifice

October 11

It was a snowy day and the sidewalk was covered with ice.

A dear little lady shuffled along, taking small careful steps.

She had on a smart woolen coat with a touch of mink at the collar and a hat to match. Her gloves were fine leather as were her shoes and pocketbook. She was going to town to shop.

As she passed by the cafe window, she slipped, and not able to react quickly enough, fell right onto her face. She looked up, pleadingly, for help.

Karen was the first to jump up. She ran out the door, and caught the little lady by the hand, helping her to her feet. The little dear immediately began brushing herself off, not realizing that her nose was broken and she was covered with blood.

She gave Karen her name and the name of her primary caregiver. Soon she was with her loved one and on her way to the doctor.

Jesus was glad that Karen helped. He is fond of that little lady.

~~~

Decide now to like strangers – while you are still young. You might be asked to care for them when they are in need, or they could end up taking care of you when you are in need.

October 12

Hope deferred makes the heart sick. *Unknown*

I pray, oh God, that I will not forget the hope I have in you, especially when...

_____

_____

_____

_____

_____
_____
_____

October 13

Obedience does not bring freedom. Freedom brings obedience. *Steve Brown*

October 14

Consider the lemon. You bang it on the counter to release the juice. You roll it and squeeze it to get out every drop of goodness. Then you add some sugar and you've got lemonade.

That's what God is doing with you, Caregiver. The process can be rough, but the reward is in becoming a mature servant who is capable and willing to spread the love. Sweet, sweet love.

October 15

An elderly Cherokee man was teaching his grandchildren about life. He said to them, "A fight is going on inside of me. It is a terrible fight. It is between two wolves. One wolf is fear, anger, envy, sorrow, regret, greed, arrogance, self-pity, guilt, resentment, inferiority, lies, false pride, superiority, and ego. The other wolf is joy, peace, love, hope, sharing, serenity, humility, kindness, benevolence, friendship, empathy, generosity, truth, compassion, and faith.

This same fight is going on inside you and inside every other person, too."

The children thought about it for a minute and then one child asked his grandfather, "Which wolf will win, Grandfather?"

The old man replied, "The one I feed."

Add to that...

Nothing is automatic about an attitude. We develop our own and it is fed and nourished by the kind of fuel we choose. *Rich Zurinsky*

~~~

The Caregiver's Formula for Success:
Godly Choices plus God's Power = Living Beyond Self

October 16

Dean was a wonderful old man. A WWII veteran, his story was both tragic and heroic. He was one of few who made it through the Bataan march. He watched many of his buddies die.

He had been shot in the groin. He was offered no medical aid. For five years Dean was imprisoned and had to serve as his own doctor. His wound never healed during the entire POW experience! But he made it back alive!

"It was the Scriptures I had memorized," he said, "that got me through each day." And every day for the rest of his life he worked on memorizing more from the Bible.

As old age took hold of Dean, he suffered a serious stroke, which disabled the right side of his body. But he would not stop!

When his caregiver, his neighbor, would come to help him get on and off the toilet, Dean would offer to display the fruits of his day's labor. "I can almost walk all the way across the living room now!" he would boast.

Eventually he made it all the way through the living room, the dining room and down the hall to his bedroom.

What a difference the Lord makes in the life of a patient! What hope Dean had! Oh, Caregiver, pray for the ones who suffer infirmity – that they might personally know the God of the Universe.

October 17

Lord, my friend asked me today if I am prepared for the death of my loved one. She warned me that I might not be.

I know that the end is near, O God; the suffering will soon be over. I am satisfied that she will be with You for all eternity. But my friend's words have caught me off guard!

I have thought of nothing else since the illness began – the unbearable pain, the anticipation of more to come – what she is going through. I have only wanted relief for her: through medication, through family comforting, and ultimately, through passing away from this life.

Have I been naive? Will I slip into self-pity at the end? Will I become concerned about my loneliness rather than her redemption?

Keep me on track, Lord. Grow me up.

October 18

Difficulties are the food of faith. *George Mueller*
This is a tough one, Lord. I really need...

_____
_____
_____
_____
_____
_____

October 19

Debbie and her dad had been through a lot together. He had beat cancer – what was it? – five times now. Strung out end-on-end, the treatments equaled five years of chemo, radiation, and surgery. Each time he pulled through.

But the news this time was: Terminal. No hope. No surgery. No treatment.

Guilt swept over Debbie. She had been there physically and emotionally for him, but not spiritually. She cried out her confession to God: "Oh, Lord, I have failed! I did not pray continually for Dad's salvation. I forgot to pray! I hoped and I wanted for him to know You, but I kept forgetting to talk to You about it!"

The following Saturday night, Debbie's dad called, "Hey, can I go to church with you tomorrow?"

This was a first!

And, of course, during that service, he went forward to surrender himself to Jesus Christ as his personal Savior and Lord.

Debbie's mustard seed had grown!

~~~

It's not how much faith you have – but Who that faith is in. Remember - it is *He* who moves mountains.

October 20

The trick is growing up without growing old. *Casey Stengel*

Have a playful day today, Caregiver! Go ahead. You deserve it!

October 21

When I am tending to the needs of one who cannot talk? And I feel lonely? Isolated? Who can I tune in to?

The soap operas? Talk shows? Reality TV?

No. I can't learn much from those.

I prefer to 'listen' to a stellar line-up of truth-tellers. Guys like David, Daniel, Solomon, Matthew, Mark, Luke, John, Paul, Peter. Now *those* guys have something to say!

October 22

Legalism, by its very nature, is always concerned with volume.

Biblical faith is always concerned with value.

Legalism will always ask, "How much?"

Christianity asks, "How so?" *Steve Brown*

Her dad had been drinking hard liquor for the past 25 years. His heart and mind were suffering in ways unimaginable. He could barely speak – his depression was so severe. He was bitter and angry.

So she had an idea. She was sure it was from the Lord! She would move her Dad in with her and wean him off alcohol. And after checking with a doctor, that is exactly what she did! She started with two beers for him in the fridge every day. Then it was one. Then it was none.

Within two months, he was drinking root beer with his dinner!

Reeling with a huge sense of accomplishment, she told a friend at church about her success.

"You mean you let him drink beer in your home?"

"Well, sure. How else could I wean him off booze? He lives with us."

"My dad is an alcoholic, too, and I have never allowed him to drink in my home."

"Well, I could hardly move Dad in and make him go cold turkey. He would have died."

"Like I said, I would NEVER allow drinking in my home. And I'm surprised you gave your dad alcohol. You should be a better witness than that!"

Grace under fire. Some people just don't get it.

October 23

Lord, he hit me today. On the arm. I cried like a baby.

Not because it hurt my arm – he's not strong enough for that anymore. He hurt my feelings. I've been on his side for three years now – as his caregiver. I feed him. I bathe him. I change his diapers.

And he hit me! Rejection!

In my recoil, I am becoming a very small package,

feeling sorry for myself.
Father, don't let me become small. Mature me.
Remind me that I have a job to do. Keep my on my
feet.

October 24

We should be like a postage stamp: sticking to one thing
– the Savior – until we get to our destination.
Knowing that You are with me blesses me when...

_____

_____

_____

_____

_____

_____

October 25

The Memory Lingers On

Sickness and old people. You know – a kid gets the flu
and he bounces back in a day or two. An elderly person
catches it, and she stays sick for days – weeks! – months!
Caregiver, have you noticed that even when the temp goes
down, the stomach relaxes, the congestion dries up, and the
doctor says she should go on vacation to Hawaii, she still sits
around in her bathrobe and asks for help in the simple tasks?
Fear is a monstrous thing.

Lord, as caregivers we fight fear every day. It is the
most serious disease of the elderly. Help us to help

*them, O God, in ways that are tangible, so that they will **live** right up until the day they die.*

October 26

A rough week for Charity. Her husband had fallen not once, but two times out of his wheelchair. He had stitches in his eyebrow as a bitter reminder.

She only looked away for a minute! But that's all it took. How he got his seatbelt off so quickly will forever be a mystery.

And now this! His feeding tube pulled right out of his stomach! Rush to the doctor! From the doctor to the hospital!

They could fix it, this time.

Charity was exhausted; she'd not had much sleep. She was perplexed; how could she continue caring for her life-long friend and lover? She was angry. *Why does he persist in fiddling with that seat belt and his feeding tube?*

The nurse overheard her under-the-breath comment: "Maybe he'll learn a lesson from this." The nurse, not understanding Charity's frustration, gave her a dirty look.

But Jesus understood. And He had no dirty looks for Charity.

He had heard the verbal requests: "Paul, please don't pull on that. Please don't fiddle with that. Honey, you'll hurt yourself."

And He had heard Charity's prayers: "Lord, help me cope. Help me be who Paul needs me to be right now. Keep me on my feet."

And He walked in her shoes with her. And when she needed, He carried her. That's what a loving God does.

Don't ever forget how much He loves you, Caregiver. You are not alone.

October 27

Both of his parents were ill: Mom, with stroke and heart failure, Dad with Alzheimer's disease. They needed full-time care.

Brent and his wife had taken them in several years before, playing the roll of full-time caregivers.

And now Dad was on his deathbed. And somehow in the fog of dementia, he remembered his role as 'father.' He leaned over, put his hand on Brent's knee and said, "Don't worry, son. Your mom will take care of you."

October 28

"What good does this bring me? The messenger is certainly harsh. But it is also a token – a love token from the King." *Unknown*

It has been tough lately, hasn't it Caregiver? You've not been appreciated. Just know that somewhere in the middle of all this, God is doing something wonderful in you!

Oh, Lord, please bring fresh encouragement to this Servant today. Amen.

October 29

Little Ruthie had never been to the roller rink before. All the people and lights and music! She squealed with delight!

She and her Auntie made their way through the crowd, Ruthie in her wheelchair, Auntie pushing behind. When they got to the edge of the rink, Ruthie got a big surprise. Auntie had purchased roller skates for her! As she put them on Ruthie's thin little feet, she talked to her niece.

"You understand, dear, that we cannot go out onto the skating rink. It would be very challenging for you to try to stand – even without the skates. Your little legs just aren't strong enough, I'm afraid. But... we will have so much fun just being here, OK?"

The manager of the rink overheard, and whispered something in Auntie's ear. Surprised, Auntie nodded an enthusiastic "Yes!"

"Ruthie, this nice man here says that he will help us put your wheelchair on the rink, and we can 'skate' around with everyone else! Isn't that great?"

And they did just that.

As they moved through the crowded arena, Auntie concentrated hard on not bumping into anyone. Ruthie, overcome with joy, expressed it by rocking her shoulders from side to side in big, happy moves.

Around and around they went. At one point, Auntie had the opportunity to glance up and what she saw amazed her. All of the people standing around the rink - adults and children alike – were rocking their shoulders in time with Ruthie's – in big, happy moves.

Lord, thank You for the encouragement for Auntie that day. Thank you for everyone who encourages a caregiver today. Amen.

October 30

If your brand of Christianity is not working at home – don't export it!

Lord, I confess that...

_____

_____

_____

_____

October 31

Every year on Halloween, Marian brought us homemade candies and caramel apples and popcorn balls. She showered us with all our favorites, "And I know Bobby likes the chocolate ones, and Johnny doesn't like those, so we have the mints for him..."

She fried up the chickens that someone left on our doorstep – knowing full well that we city folk didn't have a clue as to what to do with live fryers.

She hid little plastic animals and soldiers around her house for when the little ones would visit.

She introduced us to the other neighbors, and bought stuff at my crystal party.

She took good care of us. It was what she did – took care of people.

She nursed her first husband, suffering from cancer, until he died. And when she remarried, they discovered – oh too soon! – her second husband had cancer as well. It was during that year that we met her. She would send hubby over to our house with homegrown tomatoes from her garden, even before we had been introduced!

Marian was a caregiver's caregiver. She wrote the book on compassion. She was the personification of selflessness. Until the day she died, she volunteered at the local senior center, "just helping out."

Oh, to be mature in purpose. Oh, to be a 'Marian'.

ELEVEN

FOCUS

We don't yet see things clearly. We're squinting in a fog,
peering through a mist. But it won't be long before
the weather clears and the sun shines bright!
We'll see it all then, see it all as clearly as God sees us,
knowing him directly just as he knows us!

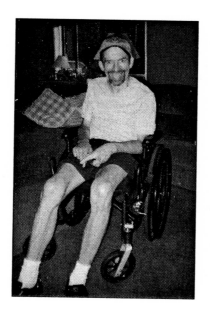

November 1

"Oh, Lord, I wish You would just send me a telegram."

Do you feel like you are seeing life through a fog? Trying to make decisions with blinders on?

In a way, that is exactly what you are doing! You cannot see the whole picture yet. But reality is there, and it will be shown – with time.

For now, the important thing is to not depend on your feelings so much (your feelings are shifting and, therefore, unreliable), as on what God tells you through His Word, the Bible. It is through learning about God's intention for you and this one you are caring for that your daily work will be affirmed.

You see, the whole package – the life, the work, the desire – is about relationship: your relationship with God; your relationship with those you care for; their relationship with God.

You can be assured that you are heading in the right direction if eternity with God is the priority.

As for the other stuff of life? Well, let the chips fall where they may.

November 2

Excited for her new psychology internship, Annie took on her job of caregiver with passion.

Children's Hospital. Troubled teens. What a challenge!

Most of the girls were on the ward for eating disorders; a couple of them had attempted suicide.

Annie anticipated long talks, where the patients would pour out their hearts and she would be able to comfort and guide them.

The girls needed the opportunity to ask – Who is God?

Does He love? Does He love *me?*

Annie wanted to explain to them that even though they could not see clearly through the fog of their emotions, they were made in God's image and they were important and loved!

It did not happen at that time and in that place because Annie was **not allowed** to talk about God. There were other more "important" things to do.

But imagine... imagine if the Great Physician had been invited in to do His healing work. The ward would have been put out of business.

November 3

There is not a king who has not had a slave among his ancestors, and there is not a slave who has not had a king in his. *Helen Keller*

Kings or slaves. It really doesn't matter, does it? Because Jesus leveled the playing field when he died for all – Prince and Pauper.

Race, Finances, Fame, Age or Infirmity. These are not factors of our worth.

Corporate Manager, Movie Star, Caregiver. All the same value.

Although, I think I heard that Caregivers pull a little more weight!

November 4

Bea had always been an individual. Which is why none of the caregivers at the nursing home were surprised at what happened.

Her family members, however, are still talking about it!

It was the Sunday before Thanksgiving. The residents' families were invited to a holiday banquet, complete with special music and a guest speaker.

Both of Bea's children and her grandchildren were in attendance. The program was progressing along nicely, when the thermostat got stuck. It became very warm in the room before the Director realized what had happened and called on the maintenance man to fix it.

In the meantime, Bea found her own solution to the heat. She politely excused herself from the table, and walker in hand, left the dinner. Her family members presumed she was going to the restroom.

When Bea returned, however, she surprised them all. She was wearing pink hot pants and cowboy boots! The outfit was topped off with a ten-gallon hat.

It remains a family mystery where she got that garb.

Who said care-giving isn't fun?

November 5

It was about midnight, and we were cruising at 34,000 feet. Mom sat next to me, holding the arm rests with a white-knuckle grip. She was afraid of many things now, including flying.

Though it was dark (the lights were out so the passengers could sleep) Mom pictured in her mind which towns, valleys and hills we were flying over. She heard a noise and 'figured' we were over Mt. Rainier.

"Oh NO!" she cried out. "We're scraping the top of the mountain!"

One by one, the reading lights throughout the aircraft went on. People jumped up, wakened by the shouting, disorientated, trying to pull themselves out of deep sleep. Adrenaline pumping.

"WHAT'S GOING ON?"

The reality was, nothing was going on. The pilot had simply put down the landing gear on our approach to Seattle.

After a few minutes of excruciating embarrassment, things settled down again, and Mom went back to her gripping.

Oh, Lord. Sometimes this one I am caring for reacts on assumptions that don't make sense. Turmoil is often the result. Steady my heart, God. Let me laugh rather than cry. Help me to stand tall, rather than shrink away in the face of chaos.

November 6

When God ordains – He sustains.

God, I praise You that You are the God of the Universe! You own the cattle on a thousand hills. You will provide when...

_____

_____

_____

_____

_____

_____

November 7

"We're being shown how to turn our backs on a godless, indulgent life, and how to take on a God-

filled, God-honoring life." Titus 2:11-13

November 8

Lord, help me not to bombard this old one with the Gospel. Give me discernment to know how much to say and when to say it. Don't let me lecture him! After all, he is 75 years old!

In Your timing and with Your wisdom give me the 'go ahead.' Then I will tell him that You are not mad at him, and that You loved him to death. Amen.

November 9

I'm running on empty. I have to dip out of everybody else's bucket. *Anonymous*

A woman, a Samaritan, came to draw water. Jesus said, "Would you give me a drink of water?" (His disciples had gone to the village to buy food for lunch.)

The Samaritan woman, taken aback, asked, "How come you, a Jew, are asking a Samaritan woman, for a drink?" (Jews in those days wouldn't be caught dead talking to Samaritans.)

Jesus answered, "If you knew the generosity of God and who I am, you would be asking me for a drink, and I would give you fresh, living water."

The woman said, "Sir you don't even have a bucket

to draw with, and this well is deep. So how are you going to get this 'living water'? ...

Jesus said, "Everyone who drinks this water will get thirsty again and again. Anyone who drinks the water I give will never thirst – not ever. The water I give will be an artesian spring within, gushing fountains of endless life. John 4:7-11,13-14

Don't you see? We're *supposed* to dip out of Someone Else's bucket!

November 10

I don't believe there really is someone called an Atheist. There are just those who are still dealing with God and they'll keep on dealing with Him until they strike the real deal – that is, complete surrender. Hopefully, it will be *before* they die.

Don't give up on this one you are caring for, dear Caregiver! Keep praying for him. He still thinks he's in charge, that's all.

November 11

This infirmed one is not the enemy. The Enemy is the enemy!

Oh, Lord, help me gain a better perspective on my work. Amen.

November 12

Sorrow looks back.
Worry looks around.
Faith looks up.

My prayer today is...

_____

_____

_____

_____

_____

_____

November 13

The question is not, "Is there a God?" The question is, "What is He like?"

You know, dear Caregiver, that others will know what God is like when they see you in your work. God is love. And you are His ambassador.

November 14

"Can you drive through the pharmacy and pick up some vitamins and my thyroid prescription?"

"Sure, Mom. Aren't you about out of your blood pressure meds, too?"

"Well, I haven't been taking those lately."

"Why not?"

"Oh, I just get tired of taking so many pills."

Lord, this is the umpteenth time we've gone through this with the meds. I get so frustrated. I want for Mom to look at the big picture. Help me have a gentle word as I talk with her again.

November 15

How many of us older persons have really been... prepared for the second half of life, for old age, death and eternity? *Carl Jung*

Dear Caregiver,

As you carry on with your chores today, remember: You are not only working on the outside, but on the inside, too! Every word, kind deed, and prayer goes straight into the heart of this suffering one. Your job is so important! You are helping to prepare another soul for eternity!

God bless you.

November 16

Many people understand the depth of their depravity. They just don't understand grace.

"[Christ] didn't, and doesn't, wait for us to get ready. He presented himself for this sacrificial death when we were far too weak and rebellious to do anything to get ourselves ready. And even if we hadn't been so weak, we wouldn't have known what to do anyway. We can understand someone dying for a person worth dying for, and we can understand how someone good and noble could

inspire us to selfless sacrifice. But God put his love on the line for us by offering his Son in sacrificial death while we were of no use whatever to him."
Romans 5:6-8

November 17

My Lord God, I have no idea where I am going. I do not see the road ahead of me, I cannot know for certain where it will end. Nor do I really know myself, and the fact that I think that I am following Your will does not mean that I am actually doing so. But I believe that the desire to please You does in fact please You. And I hope I have that desire in all that I am doing. I hope that I will never do anything apart from that desire. And I know that if I do this You will lead me by the right road though I may know nothing about it. Therefore I will trust You always though I may seem to be lost and in the shadow of death. I will not fear, for You are ever with me, and You will never leave me to face my perils alone. *Thomas Merton* [17]

November 18

The difference between the impossible and the possible lies in determination. *Tommy Lasorda*
I need a different outlook, Lord. I'm concerned about...

_____

_____

_____

_____

_____

_____

November 19

"The fundamental fact of existence is that this trust in God, this faith, is the firm foundation under everything that makes life worth living. It's our handle on what we can't see. The act of faith is what distinguished our ancestors, set them above the crowd." Hebrews 11:1

November 20

Guilt has only one purpose – and that is to draw us to Jesus. *Steve Brown*

O soul, are you weary and troubled?
No light in the darkness you see?
There's light for a look at the Savior,
And life more abundant and free!

Turn your eyes upon Jesus,
Look full in His wonderful face,
And the things of earth will grow strangely dim
In the light of His glory and grace. *Helen H. Lemmel* [18]

November 21

He could no longer tie his shoes. He could not figure out how to use a toothbrush.

But he was incredibly perceptive:

When his granddaughter broke up with her boyfriend... "She has sad eyes."

When he was started on new meds... "Pills are making me tired."

When his son-in-law quit work to care for him... "The boss is here! He's a good man."

He still understood some things. How exciting!

It was not too late to talk with him about Jesus, after all!

November 22

Both father and son were having a wonderful day! Cruising at 7,000 feet in their fast little sport plane, they buzzed over the fields and hilltops with abandon. Right up until the engine died.

Keeping their wits about them, each did his job with perfection. Dad steadied the rate of descent while Johnny looked for a field to land on.

They spotted a private airstrip and glided in – no muss – no fuss.

Wouldn't it be nice if all emergencies in life were handled so smoothly?

But in your line of work, Caregiver, you are often the only one in the room who can think clearly enough to focus on what is important. Sometimes, too, the smallest incident can become bigger than life for the one you are caring for.

You may not have the option of a smooth ride every day. But you do have the power of love to keep you aloft. And love cushions even the bumpiest of flights!

November 23

She had had her feelings hurt so many times – she felt too inadequate to help anybody.

"It's just the opposite!" cried her friend. "Maybe bruised, now you can be used!"

Lord, take the painful experience of my past and use it to help this hurting one now. Take what Satan intended for evil and turn it into good. Make me a caregiver.

Amen.

November 24

Think of all the beauty still left around you and be happy. *Anne Frank*

Lord, I cannot deny the necessity of pain and suffering in life. How else would we learn to depend on You? But also, Lord, help me to see the beauty in...

_____

_____

_____

_____

_____

_____

November 25

The brave are simply those with the clearest vision of what is before them – glory and danger alike – and notwithstanding, go out to meet it. (*in the movie "Kate & Leopold"*)

Ruthie and her daddy had a date. These times together were a joy! And, they were a challenge.

Bound to her wheelchair, and having very little control over her body, the outings had to be orchestrated so that Ruthie's comfort was not threatened in any way. Otherwise, it would not be fun!

Dad decided to take his little girl out for a big treat: They would visit the waterfront with all its activity and noise and nature. Then, to top off the event, they would eat at a fancy-schmancy restaurant.

Sighting a great place on the water – this was the perfect spot! – Dad looked the menu over to make sure there were an appropriate number of kids' items on it: hamburgers, fish and chips, etc.

Ruthie, however, chose some different options. Working with her trembling hands, struggling to get them to cooperate, she pointed to the items *she* wanted to try on the menu. She ate 3 oysters on the half shell, 3 oysters Rockefeller, an entire Waldorf salad, a huge piece of salmon and a slab of chocolate cake! There was not a soul in the place that was not touched by Ruthie's infirmity and her bravery.

As she was wheeled out, the entire staff including the maitre d', lined up to pat her on the head, shake her little hand, and bid her adieu.

On that cool waterfront evening many, many Seattle hearts were warmed.

November 26

Social workers. Ya gotta love 'em. They are doing their best – they really are – but sometimes, WOW!

Take the thirty-year-old gal who would not let Dad out of the hospital until I attended 'feeding' lessons with him. I learned all the little tricks about where to poke and prod so that he would swallow, but the truth of it was – he *couldn't* swallow anymore! No matter, I had to take the lessons.

Then there was the one who wouldn't let us give Dad a certain tranquilizer to calm his hallucinations. She said it was too addictive. So we had to switch meds. No matter that he was on his deathbed.

We get frustrated with those in authority, don't we, Caregiver? In many cases we're older than them and understand the situation better than them.

We will feel a lot better if we remember this: None of us sees all things clearly! Only God does. In areas where we 'get it,' others may not. And when we are totally blinded, someone else may have better glasses on. Often – *all* of us are walking around in a fog together.

Somehow it all works together for good when we trust in Him.

November 27

> *"But God is doing what is best for us, training us to live God's holy best. At the time, discipline isn't much fun. It always feels like it's going against the grain. Later, of course, it pays off handsomely, for it's the well-trained who find themselves mature in their relationship with God.*
>
> *"So don't sit around on your hands! No more dragging your feet! Clear the path for long-distance runners so no one will trip and fall, so no one will step in a hole and sprain an ankle. Help each other out. And run for it!" Hebrews 12:13*

November 28

Jennifer always had to sit in the front row at school. Even then, she could not see the blackboard. She saw the things of life in a fog. The eldest of nine children, she just didn't feel justified in asking for glasses.

Her mom was sick – Schizophrenia – and her dad

worked long hours to keep food on the table, so Jennifer didn't get the attention she needed.

As Jennifer's teacher, I finally asked for a conference with the parents, and requested that they invest in reading glasses for the girl.

"Oh, Mrs. Z!" she declared on her first day with glasses. "I got out of the car, and I was just staring up at the trees. I had never seen individual leaves before! As I was looking up, I walked right into the drainage ditch at the side of our driveway!" We shared a good laugh together.

A few years later, I ran into Jennifer again. She was suffering from mental illness. Again, nobody noticed soon enough to get her the help that she needed. Her mother had run off with half of the children, and her father was still working long hours. She had had to quit high school to care for her younger siblings. Her dreams of becoming a doctor were down the tube.

But it was worse than that. She had become dependent on anti-depressant, anti-hallucinogenic, anti-psychotic and anti-anxiety drugs to name a few. She was taking about fourteen pills a day – just to temper her personality! Once again, she was seeing life in a fog.

We attempted to be the caregivers for Jennifer. We contacted all of her doctors and previous caregivers for consultation. We contacted her family church. Everyone had given up hope.

But they weren't bad people. And they weren't wimps. We found that out. After several attempts at suicide, we realized that we, too, would not be able to help Jennifer safely.

It's OK, Caregiver. Sometimes your heart says "yes" but the patient, in a manner of speaking, says "no." You must let go.

November 29

Grandma had always wanted to go to Hawaii. A couple of years after Grandpa died, the family took her there. Such a beautiful place! So many sights to see! But Grandma could not enjoy it to the fullest measure because she was going blind. She had macular degeneration, which prevented her from seeing what was directly in front of her.

The walks on the beach did not mean as much as they might have years ago. Walking through the botanical gardens did not bring as much pleasure as we had hoped. "I just can't see a thing," she complained. Eventually Grandma became irritable and preferred napping to sightseeing.

Then, her son-in-law had an idea. "Mom," he said, "let's go see Don Ho!"

Well, she picked right up! A real singing star! Now *that* would be something to talk about when she got home!

The concert went as expected. Don Ho sang several old standards, and ended up with "Tiny Bubbles." The crowd responded enthusiastically. Then, something *unexpected* happened. Mr. Ho invited all the grandmothers to join him up on the stage.

The family was sitting up on a second tier in the dining club. It would be difficult for them to guide Grandma through two levels of seating. But, no bother. Before anyone could assist her, she was up and winding through the crowd alone.

She was one of the first grandmas on the stage, and Don Ho gave her a big kiss on the cheek! Beaming, she made her way back to the table.

This blind little old lady got where she wanted to go. She followed his voice!

There is a truth here. We often see what we want to see. And whoever beckons us – who we listen to — determines what path we will follow.

"By your words I can see where I'm going; they throw a beam of light on my dark path." Psalms 119:105

November 30

We set the sail – God makes the wind.
Lord, I need a big push, because...

_____

_____

_____

_____

_____

_____

TWELVE

PAUSE

But for right now, until that completeness, we have three things to do to lead us toward that consummation: Trust steadily in God, hope unswervingly, love extravagantly. And the best of the three is love.

December 1

"So, did I do good?" "Did I do an OK job?"

Do you find yourself seeking answers to these questions?

It's not that you want people to praise you or applaud you. It's just that you want to know – Have you been affective in your ministry of care-giving? Have you loved?

The one you have taken care of may not be able to answer you. And nobody else has been around 24/7 to give an accurate appraisal.

Except God, that is. He has been watching full-time.

He would answer your questions with some questions of His own:

- Did you have faith in Me?
- Did you hope for the eternal best?
- Did you love this other one as much as you love yourself?

If you can answer Yes! Yes! Yes! – you did well.

You see, it is all about *His* perspective!

December 2

I will sing of Your mercy that brings me through valleys of sorrow to rivers of joy. *Jars of Clay*

"Consider it a sheer gift, friends, when tests and challenges come at you from all sides. You know that under pressure, your faith-life is forced into the open and shows its true colors. So don't try to get out of anything prematurely. Let it do its work so you become mature and well-developed, not

deficient in any way." James 1:2-4

December 3

The staff had been waiting for this for five years: Their new building. A place where they could work and their residents could live in style.

It was a brand-spankin' new assisted-living home. It had all of the amenities: perfect lighting, good food, and spacious rooms. The staff was energetic! What a facility!

During the Grand Opening, however, they discovered that they had not quite sharpened every pencil. With all their experience, they had somehow forgotten to put a gate at the top of a small staircase.

Gertrude, a resident in the old building for almost seven years, sat in her wheelchair at the top of the new stairs. She had not moved on her own in all the time they had known her. She sat rigidly, back straight, hands gripping the arm-rests, eyes straight ahead, pursed lips. When it was time to bathe her or put her to bed, they had to literally pry her body out of the chair and onto the shower seat or into her bed-clothes.

But tonight Gertrude decided to do something on her own. She reached down and pushed on the wheel of her chair – just enough to send her flying down the stairs! The chair caught on the rail halfway, and she rolled out and somersaulted the rest of the way down.

"Glad you could drop in, Gert," joked one startled care-giver. Probably not the most appropriate response, but Gertrude liked it. She turned her head, looked up and smiled!

There was no anger. There would be no repercussion this time.

Lord, we make mistakes! Keep us alert as we stumble through this process of care-giving. Every day is a new adventure, God, and we need Your protection. Amen.

December 4

The old gentlemen said, "I'm going to die and I'm going to hell."

His caregiver, rather than acting 'shocked' replied calmly, "We are all going to die, Mr. Jones. And you do not have to go to hell. Do you know why?" and proceeded to tell him about Jesus.

The old fellow just hadn't understood his options. He thought there was too much water under the bridge. But we know, don't we? It's never too late!

"God rescued us from dead-end alleys and dark dungeons. He's set us up in the kingdom of the Son he loves so much, the Son who got us out of the pit we were in, got rid of the sins we were doomed to keep repeating." Colossians 1:13-14

December 5

The folks in the Alzheimer's unit were restless that day. Only three or four of them were being entertained by the craft project. But their new caregiver would not give up on them.

When the head nurse came to check on them, she found a particularly happy group.

"What have you done? Why are they all so cheerful?"

"We've been dancing," came the reply, as the caregiver

rubbed her thighs.

"Dancing?"

"Oh, yeah," said the caregiver. "We sat in our seats and let 'er rip for over an hour! It was hard – but it sure was worth it!"

What a great caregiver! What a novel idea! Unconventional – but it worked! The proof is in the puddin'.

December 6

Consider, friends, as you pass by, as you are now, so once was I.

As I am now, you too shall be. Prepare, therefore, to follow me.

(*Scottish Tombstone Epitaph*)

Amazing, isn't it? The connections we have with one another. Besides death, there is...

_____

_____

_____

_____

_____

_____

December 7

Don't panic!

God's work
Done God's way
Will not lack

God's provision.

December 8

It seems to me age can make people softer inside just as it makes your skin softer – as if the soft pliant skin on the outside is a physical expression of a new give inside, in the personality...The urgencies of yesterday have fallen away, the demand for this or that concrete objective evaporates, and what is left is the most patient and well-meaning you. *Peggy Noonan* [19]

> *Lord, I thank you that I have this elderly one to care for. Amen.*

December 9

Looking back through history you can see the baton being passed through various hands, and the only sure thing is the baton. *Sylvia Jacobson*

Right now, Caregiver, *you* are carrying the baton - the wand of the Word of the Gospel. And what you do with it will influence many generations to come.

December 10

Paul insists on eating with the family, even though his esophagus no longer functions normally. He has to regurgitate most of what he swallows. He does not understand that this makes a whole lot of work for his wife, his caregiver. In his desperation hold on life, he is wrapped up in continuing to do what he has always been able to do. And the fact the she has to change his clothing several times a day does not impress him. He does not want to totally depend on a feeding tube!

Paul is a wonderful guy who has a terrible disease. His wife, Charity, is a wonderful lady, who cannot feel his pain no matter how hard she tries.

In their separate thoughts, they are not able to fully see the situation. As a team, they depend on God to clear things up eventually - in eternity.

Oh, Lord, as a caregiver, I don't always see the big picture. And I cannot make all the tough decisions by myself. What I decide totally affects the one I care for. The responsibility is overwhelming, Father. I'm so glad You are here.

December 11

A family altar can alter a family.

December 12

Truth, unlike beauty, is NOT in the eye of the beholder. *Selected*

My prayer, Lord, is that I will see things the way they really are. And then I can pass the truth on to...

_____

_____

_____

_____

_____

_____

December 13

"Don't fool yourself. Don't think that you can be wise merely by being up-to-date with the times. Be God's fool – that's the path to true wisdom. What the world calls smart, God calls stupid. It's written in Scripture,

He exposes the chicanery of the chic.
The Master sees through the smoke screens of the know-it-alls." 1 Corinthians 3:19

Father, keep me humble. Allow me to seek Your wisdom and not my own as I serve as a caregiver. Because really, Lord, what do I know? Amen.

December 14

Lord Jesus,

When I meet You today in your unattractive disguise of the irritating, the exacting and the unreasonable, may I still recognize You and say, "Sweet Jesus, what a privilege it is to serve you today." *Mother Theresa of Calcutta*

December 15

River. What a great name for a little boy. River. How unique.

His parents did not know when they gave him the name just how telling it was.

Things went well with the pregnancy and delivery. His first few months were great. But then River slowed in his progress toward crawling and walking. Something was going terribly wrong!

Grandmothers were consulted. There was one doctor visit after another. No one could sort it out.

As River physically grew, mentally he seemed to withdraw. Then, the appropriate diagnosis: River had autism. He did not walk. He did not speak.

He had no desire to join in with his surroundings.

But River's family was full of love. Love for River and love for God. And love... well, in this case... Love...conquered all.

River's family took the matter in hand. Praying 24/7 they worked with him. They played with him, snuggled with him, and attempted to communicate with him beyond normal endurance.

Now, at five years old, River has fixated on life around him, rather than life within him!

He is determined to join in. He must go swimming with Grandma and Grandpa! He must help his mama in the kitchen. He must get to church on time!

This precious little boy is indeed a river: of joy, exuberance, of life!

December 16

...learning how to live necessarily involves a good deal of meditation on and consideration of death. If we don't give our full attention to death, but spend our lives avoiding the subject and obscuring it with euphemisms, we diminish our lives. Denial of death is avoidance of life. It's significant that in telling us the story of Jesus – a story that has more life in it than any other – the four Gospel Evangelists provide us with far more details about Jesus' dying and death than any other aspect of his life. *Eugene Peterson* [20]

Thank You, Lord Jesus, for showing us how to live ***and*** *how to die.*

December 17

This is a faith of feet. *Rich Zurinsky*

How beautiful on the mountains
are the feet of the messenger bringing good news,
Breaking the news that all's well,
proclaiming good times, announcing salvation,
telling Zion, "Your God reigns!" Isaiah 52:7

Hey, Caregiver! Time to show and tell!

December 18

God wisely designed the human body so that we can neither pat our own backs nor kick ourselves too easily.

I praise You, God – for we are wonderfully made! You don't make mistakes! Help me to remember that when...

_____

_____

_____

_____

_____

_____

December 19

"The truth of the matter is that you always know the

right thing to do. The hardest part is doing it." *General Norman Schwarzkopf*

Lord, lead me in the right way today. Make my intentions Your intentions. My words Your words. My heart Your heart. Amen.

December 20

I dreaded the visit I was about to make. As I crossed over the threshold I carried with me the burden of extreme sadness, for Roberta was dying a painful and terrible death.

Catching me off guard, the room resounded with the ring of laughter. Was she laughing out loud? This widow of six years? The one who had had to find a Christian home for her four children before she could go? Laughing?

Soon I was caught up in the unexplainable joy of Roberta. I helped her wrap the Christmas gifts that she had ordered for her children. She smiled often, imagining the broad grins of each one as they opened their presents.

She possessed a peace that passes understanding. She was a lover of Jesus.

On Christmas Eve, we sang to her and prayed for her, and in the wee hours the next morning, secure in the knowledge that her children would be taken care of, Roberta went home to be with her Lord. No more pain. No more suffering.

As I reflect on that wrapping day so long ago, I realize that no matter who was watching Roberta, *she* was the caregiver in the room!

December 21
First Day of Winter

Grandpa was a busy man. He worked full-time at the copper smelter. He also ran the family farm.

At Christmas however, he found time to spend with us.

"Time to get the tree!" he would announce. And off we'd go – trudging through the snow – on our annual hunt for the perfect Christmas decoration.

It took all day; sometimes two trips out. Grandpa showed us his love by giving us the gift of his time.

Can I do any less for him now?

December 22

Ha! A Success!

He hadn't been to church in 35 years. God had disappointed him somewhere along the way. And he was shaking his fist at the Creator of the Universe.

Then he became ill. He put himself in the care of others. He began to notice that the ones who were showing him concern – granting him dignity – were getting through each day prayerfully, as if holding God's hand.

Eventually, his anger eased, and he began to understand love. The love he had been missing: The love of others, the love of God.

His communication skills were naught, but his message came through loud and clear one day...

"Who is God, Dad?"

"He takes care..."

"He takes care of you?"

"Oh, yes!"

"Do you know that He loves you?"

"Well, certainly!"

(Like Ronald Reagan used to say. It was that "small moment with a big meaning.")

December 23

The Christmas Cruise – we had watched it from afar for many years.

"Aren't the yachts beautiful?"

"Look how they are all lit up."

"I wonder why they do this each year?"

"Are they just showing off?"

Until one year when we were invited to participate. Not that we had a yacht. But we did live across the street from the Yacht Club cabana.

We were assigned dock duty. Our entire job was to point the way to the boarding ramp – making sure that the passengers did not make a bad turn and fall into the drink.

"See Santa Claus up there? Just walk toward him. He'll help you get on the boat."

The passengers were not your typical yachting set. They were the local tenants of the group homes: the mentally challenged, the physically handicapped, and their caregivers.

It was all so clear. Yes! The yacht owners *were* showing off! They were showing off compassion, patience and love.

Lord, let me use what I have to touch others today. As this Christmas season is upon us, with all its trimmings, remind me to use these luxuries for You. Amen.

December 24

We're naked, unfettered, unfinished, unprotected – if we don't have Christ on. *Steve Brown*

What comfort to know Your love, Father! Remind me that You are there, will you Lord? Especially when...

December 25
Christmas Day

The Most Awesome Caregiver of All

"For a child has been born – for us!
the gift of a son – for us!
He'll take over
the running of the world.
His names will be: Amazing Counselor,
Strong God,
Eternal Father,
Prince of Wholeness." Isaiah 9:6

December 26

I used to ask God to help me.
Then I asked if I might help Him.
I ended up by asking God to do His work through me.
Hudson Taylor

December 27

Grandma's recipe for syrup:

2 Cups Sugar
1 Cup Water
2 Tablespoons Corn Syrup
1 Tablespoon Maple Flavoring
1 Teaspoon Vanilla

Have granddaughter mix all ingredients in big pot over open-flame stove, stirring continually while you sing and tell stories and flip the hotcakes – the thin batter dollar-size ones, of course – on another burner.

Serve up with lots of love and laughter.
Cost? Your time.
Benefit? Immeasurable.

Lord, as I care for this dear one, I am reminded that she is someone's Grandma. I sense that in the past she has given her time for a loved one. I ask that I would love her as I spend time with her today.

December 28

Moses spent 40 years being a 'somebody,'
40 years (hiding out) being a 'nobody,'
And the next 40 years seeing what
God can do with a 'nobody.'

December 29

It's not over 'til it's over.

The kids had come home from college to help take care of Grandpa in his dying days. Together with their dad, they bathed him and fed him and read to him and sang to him. They held his hand when he looked frightened and they prayed over him.

He slipped into a coma and they continued to keep him clean and medicated. It was a grueling time. They did not sleep the last night, but stayed by his side so that **if** he could still hear them, still be aware of them, he would have the knowledge that he was being taken care of.

When he slipped into eternity, they were there, and they continued to care for him.

"He's not going out of here in a diaper."

They bathed him one last time, put clean and pressed clothes on him, combed his hair and allowed my last vision of him to be a dignified one.

Oh, Caregiver, it's so important to finish the job.

December 30

He takes my finger and He won't let go. *Newsboys*

Stalwart walks in step with God;
his path blazed by God, he's happy.
If he stumbles, he's not down for long;
God has a grip on his hand. Psalm 37:23-24

Oh God, I need you to hold my hand because...

_____

_____

_____

_____

_____

December 31

Perspective.

Wally Cox said that when he bought a newspaper, he would take it home, put it in the drawer for two weeks, then read it and say, "Wow! I'm glad we're not going through that anymore!"

Father, as I look back on my year, help me to read hope into the successes and the mishaps. Allow me to recognize You in the shaping of events. Then, O God, give me a grateful heart. Amen.

NOTES...

1. Margaret Denison Armstrong, poet, evangelistic singer, overseas missionary.

2. Darrell Evans, *Trading My Sorrows.* Used with permission.

3. Thomas Merton as quoted by Henri J.M. Nouwen, *Aging: The Fulfillment of Life* (New York: Bantam Doubleday Dell Publishing Group, 1974), p.114.

4. Twila Paris, *Same Girl.* Used with permission.

5. Henri J.M. Nouwen, *Our Greatest Gift: A Meditation on Dying and Caring* (New York: HarperCollins, 1997), p.10.

6. Ibid., pp. 20,21.

7. Henri J.M. Nouwen, *Aging: The Fulfillment of Life,* p. 77.

8. A. Wetherell Johnson, *Created for Commitment* (Carol Stream, Illinois: Tyndale House, 1989).

9. Edited by Thomas H. Johnson, *The Complete Poems*

of Emily Dickinson (New York: Little, Brown and Company, 1961), p. 339. Used by permission from Harvard University Press.

10. H. Ruby, R. Bloom, *Give Me the Simple Life.* Used with permission.

11. Thomas H. Johnson, op. cit., p. 616.

12. Eugene H. Peterson, *Leap Over a Wall: Earthy Spirituality for Everyday Christians* (New York: HarperCollins, 1997), p. 219.

13. McGuffey's Second Reader, as quoted by William J. Bennett, *The Book of Virtues* (New York: Simon & Schuster, 1993), p.134.

14. Matt Redman, *Blessed Be the Name.* Used with permission.

15. Henri J.M. Nouwen, *Our Greatest Gift: A Meditation on Dying and Caring,* p. 67.

16. Robert E. Mickelson, *When Was That Moment?*

17. Thomas Merton, *Thoughts in Solitude* (New York: Dell, 1961), p. 79.

18. Helen Lemmel, *Turn Your Eyes Upon Jesus.* Used with permission.

19. Peggy Noonan, *When Character Was King* (New York: Penguin Group, 2001), p. 7.

20. Peterson, op. cit., p. 218.

Reasonable care has been taken to trace ownership and, when necessary, obtain permission for each selection included.

Acknowledgments

Many gifted individuals have served God well in the area of care-giving. Loving, generous people. I am grateful to those who have chosen to share their stories with me. Without you, this book would not have been possible.

Thank you to the Hayes family, the McIntoshes, the DeFronzos, the Howers, Dottie Bell, Cher Fleener, the Miller family, my mom, Barbara, and all the Mickelsons, the Allens, Paula Wilz, the Abells, the Hobbs, Sandie Carr, Audrey Turco, the Salzwedels, Virginia Blair, Cherie Franich, the Christy family, the Mississippi Zurinskys, and of course, my *own* Zurinskys – Rich, Bob, Anne & John. Beloved Caregivers all.

Also thank you to the folks at Port Orchard Care, Orchard Pointe Memory Care, Harrison Hospital, The Doctors Clinic, and Hospice for their kind service to my family in our time of need.

And to Dr. Steve Brown, Key Life Ministries, whose teachings have encouraged me beyond measure.

God bless you all!

Laurie Zurinsky